CAKEOLOGY

*To Simon, Lydia,
Ruby and George*

Juliet Sear

CAKEOLOGY

PHOTOGRAPHY BY

Helen Cathcart

CONTENTS

FOREWORD 06

WELCOME TO CAKEOLOGY 09

1. TOOLKIT 13

DO NOT START THE PROJECTS BEFORE READING THIS! 23

2. PROJECTS 25

Vase & Flowers INTERMEDIATE/ADVANCED 26
Cupcake Bouquet EASY/INTERMEDIATE 33
Tattooed Sailor Nautical Cookie Explosion INTERMEDIATE 36
Monochrome Chevron Cake INTERMEDIATE/ADVANCED 45
Framed Insect Taxidermy INTERMEDIATE/ADVANCED 50
Old-School Trainer ADVANCED 57
Lydia's Loveheart Cookies EASY 62
Celebrookies INTERMEDIATE 69
Wedgwood-Inspired White-on-White Wedding Cake INTERMEDIATE/ADVANCED 72
Not-So-Dirty Burger INTERMEDIATE/ADVANCED 79
Painted & Printed Birds EASY/INTERMEDIATE 84
'World's Best Dad' Chocolate Mini Bites EASY 88
Piñata Surprise EASY 92
Sea Salted Caramel Seaside Cupcakes EASY 99
Doggy Biscuits EASY 104
Acid Brights Buttercream Cake INTERMEDIATE 109
Christmas Snowmen Mini Cakes EASY/INTERMEDIATE 114
Mexican Skull INTERMEDIATE/ADVANCED 119
Christmas Kitsch Cookies INTERMEDIATE 122
Club Tropicana INTERMEDIATE/ADVANCED 127
Stencil Cowboy Cake EASY/INTERMEDIATE 134
Vintage Floral Patchwork Cake ADVANCED 139
Woodland Creatures Fondant Cupcakes INTERMEDIATE 146
Muliti-Chocolate Rose Cake ADVANCED 153

3. THE BASICS: (Technical Jargon; Cake Preparation; Splitting, Filling & Covering Cakes;
Cake Building; Decorating with Royal Icing) 157

4. RECIPES 199

THANK YOUS 230

ABOUT THE AUTHOR 232

INDEX 234

FOREWORD

~~~

I first met Juliet Sear in 2013 when she came over to New Jersey to work with me and the team at Carlos Bakery. We immediately hit it off – her passion, humour and professionalism made her easy to work with.

Anyone who has watched Cake Boss will know that innovative, creative cake designs and *la mia famiglia* – my family – are the most important things to me, and in **Cakeology** both of these things are in abundance. Juliet's energy and enthusiasm for cakes is infectious, and since that first meeting she has become the European ambassador for my Cake Boss range of baking and decorating equipment.

I like the project-style step-by-step approach of Juliet's book, not only because it will help home bakers to replicate many of the cool designs inside, it will also inspire them to change and adapt the projects to make their own personalised cakes for friends and family. Juliet's writing style is easy for people to follow, and I am sure with her guidance readers will be able to achieve a professional finish with their cakes at home.

There's lots in here for beginners to start out with – the simple decorated cookies, ganache mini cakes and the piñata cake – through to the more advanced cakes, like multi-tiered designs and sculptural cakes which are a little more challenging. I love making stunning cakes that tempt people's taste buds and treat their eyes, and Juliet's recipes and cake projects will have you creating exciting cakes that also taste scrumptious!

Whether you want to create an amazing birthday cake for your best friend or spend time in the kitchen with the kids, I know this book will inspire you and teach you something new. What are you waiting for? Go have some fun!

Buddy Valastro

Buddy Valastro
CAKE BOSS

WELCOME TO

~~~

CAKEOLOGY

I have been immersed in the world of baking and cake decoration for over a decade. As well as running my own cake boutique I have had the opportunity to work creatively with many global brands and high-profile clients all looking to push cake design beyond the usual. With so many people making cakes these days my clients want me to come up with something that stands out from the crowd, and rising to this challenge is what I love best.

Everywhere I look I see cake: not just on cookery TV shows but across social media, such as Pinterest and Instagram, where beautiful cake designs frequently catch my eye. With so much inspiration, I find I constantly want to experiment with new designs that stretch my skills and ability. Cake decorating can be quite addictive – once you get started, you can't get enough. It can also get very competitive!

The projects in this book are tailored to take you, too, beyond the basics of baking and cake decorating, into the realm where cake design merges with the wonderful world of arts and crafts, offering endless scope for innovation and surprise. With this in mind, I have incorporated a wide range of techniques that you can use to manipulate and adapt the projects to make them your own, or use as a creative springboard to create magical new designs. I hope they will challenge and inspire everyone, from the beginner to the more accomplished among you.

By sharing the creative process behind the projects, oodles of practical know-how, as well as insider tips and tricks, you can start to have fun creating your own masterpieces. The freedom of the creative process should be part of the joy; for me, a dose of kitchen-art therapy works wonders as a distraction from the stresses of a hectic schedule.

I often teach the art of cake decorating in the classroom and at live demonstrations, and nothing is more rewarding than seeing others inspired and delighted by the results. My hope is that through this book I can pass a little bit of that joy and fun on to you.

GOOD LUCK, AND HAPPY BAKING!

Juliet Sear

DIFFICULTY GUIDE

For the Projects section

~~~

Easy

Easy / Intermediate

Intermediate

Intermediate / Advanced

Advanced

SECTION ONE

TOOLKIT

*Advice on the kit you need
to create beautiful cakes*

BAKING KIT

There is an abundance of innovative and helpful cake-decorating and baking tools available now, particularly since the huge surge of interest in homebaking over the past 10 years. Of course, you can decorate a cake beautifully with a minimum amount of fancy kit, but if you want to increase your repertoire, and make the job easier and quicker, you can order all sorts of handy tools from around the globe and have them delivered to your door. The US is a great source: I recently lost several hours in the NY Cake Shop in New York with our daughter Lydia, emerging with over $500 of stuff that I couldn't get here in the UK (I could have spent a whole lot more, but not without my husband Simon having a heart attack!).

There is also a wide variety of cool edible supplies that you can use to 'pimp up' your cakes, ranging from gorgeous glitters, gems and adornments in every colour imaginable, to sugar decorations in hundreds of shapes, sizes and colours, edible prints, and metallic embellishments.

If you haven't got certain pieces of equipment, there are handy things you can substitute. When we have many cakes on the go at Fancy Nancy we run out of kit so have to resort to ingenious ways of replacing equipment; for example, an upturned cake tin, book or bowl works as a makeshift turntable. If you are just starting out, you might not want to splash your cash on tools, so where I can I've offered tips for how you might improvise with everyday kit already in your kitchen.

ESSENTIALS:

ELECTRIC STAND MIXER: e.g. Kitchen Aid. This is my favourite piece of kit. They are real workhorses and although you can do without one or use a hand-held electric mixer instead, they make cake making and decorating much quicker.

DIGITAL SCALES

SPATULA

SPOONS: wooden spoons; large metal tablespoon.

KNIVES: large serrated bread knife for cutting, splitting and filling cakes; small, sharp knife.

PALETTE KNIVES: large, medium and small, for covering, spreading and lifting cakes.

CAKE LEVELLER

CAKE TINS IN VARIOUS SIZES & SHAPES: I use standard professional cake tins that are 7.5 cm (3 in) deep. You can use any tin, but always plan the final height of your layered cake.

MUFFIN TRAYS

MUFFIN CASES

COOKIE CUTTERS: can also be used to cut sugarpaste.

COOKIE STICKS: for making cookie lollipops.

NON-STICK BAKING PARCHMENT OR PAPER

SCISSORS

PASTRY BRUSH

NOTE › *All the recipes in this book have been tested in a fan-assisted oven. If you are using a conventional oven, increase the oven temperature by 20°C (70°F). An oven thermometer is a useful tool if you are a keen baker, as thermostats on domestic ovens can be inaccurate.*

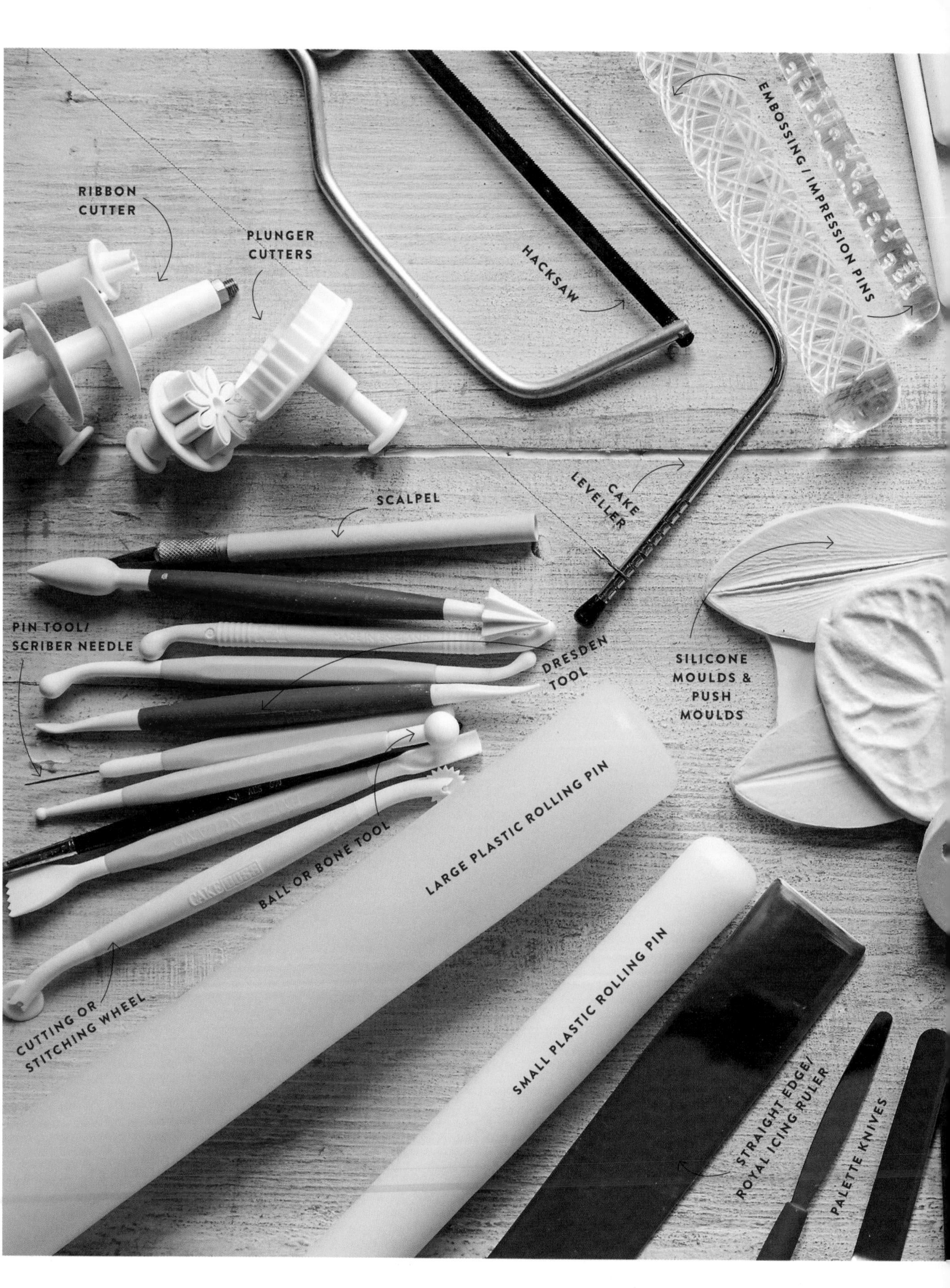

RIBBON
CUTTER

PLUNGER
CUTTERS

HACKSAW

EMBOSSING / IMPRESSION PINS

SCALPEL

CAKE
LEVELLER

PIN TOOL/
SCRIBER NEEDLE

DRESDEN
TOOL

SILICONE
MOULDS &
PUSH
MOULDS

BALL OR BONE TOOL

LARGE PLASTIC ROLLING PIN

CUTTING OR
STITCHING WHEEL

SMALL PLASTIC ROLLING PIN

STRAIGHT EDGE/
ROYAL ICING RULER

PALETTE KNIVES

CAKE DOWELS

GUIDE STICKS

PIPING
TUBES &
NOZZLES

CAKE SMOOTHERS

ROSE
CUTTER

SIDE SCRAPER

IMPRESSION MATS

TWEEZERS

CAKE-DECORATING KIT

ESSENTIALS:

LARGE PLASTIC ROLLING PIN
CAKE SMOOTHERS: ideally
two side smoothers and one top
smoother. A side smoother has a
straight side and top smoothers have
completely rounded edges to prevent
digging into the surface of the cake
when polishing.

CAKE BOARDS
PIPING BAGS
BLADE & SHELL TOOL
BALL OR BONE TOOL
DRESDEN TOOL
SCALPEL
PIPING TUBES/NOZZLES

NICE BUT NOT NECESSARY:

SCRIBER NEEDLE OR PIN TOOL: used to
pop air bubbles, remove tiny particles or colour
marks, and for marking out lettering/patterns on a
cake. (You can use a regular ball-head pin instead)

MODELLING TOOL: there are many different
ones for shaping and sculpting, including
Dresden, bone, blade and shell tools. When I
worked in Buddy Valastro's (AKA the Cake Boss)
amazing bakery, his extremely talented model
makers were using dental tools for cake work!
They're brilliant – I bought a set of 12 online for
just £5.49.

PROJECTOR: some people like to project
images onto a cake surface to aid hand-painting
or piping. It's great if you are not good at free-
hand drawing and painting. Alternatively, you
can print a picture from the computer and mark
out the edges by stabbing through the paper
to create a dotted line on the icing, then all you
have to do is 'join the dots' with icing!

TURNTABLE: a really handy aid for cake
decorating. Alternatively, use a TV swivel stand
(can be found online for around £5 – just google
'revolving TV turntable'), which can take a larger
cake weight than a standard cake turntable, or

substitute with an upturned cake tin sitting on a
tea towel, or a thick cookery book wrapped in
foil to elevate your cake.

TILTING TURNTABLE: a professional
turntable that also has a tilting mechanism and
non-slip surface so you can angle the cake. This
makes intricate piping on the side of a cake so
much easier.

GUIDE STICKS OR MARZIPAN SPACERS

CAKE DRUMS: thick foil-covered cake boards
that sit under sponges, or can be used as iced
stands for display. They're also useful as a guide to
smooth against when using cake smoothers.

CAKE CARDS: thinner than cake drums,
cheaper, not such good quality but handy for
smaller cakes or less heavy dowelled cakes.

SIDE SCRAPER: you can use a small plastic
ruler if you haven't got one.

STRAIGHT EDGE: you can use a metal or
strong plastic ruler instead, but these generally
only go up to 30 cm (12 in) so you can't use
these for cakes that are bigger than this.

NOTE

〜

Make sure when you buy a
nozzle set that it includes
No. 2 and No. 3 round
nozzles, and a star nozzle.

RIBBON CUTTER: a handy wheeled cutter that can be adjusted to cut different widths of sugarpaste, chocolate or petal paste.

CAKE DOWELS FOR STACKING CAKES: extra-strong heavy-duty dowels are ideal, especially for your base cake if you are creating a stacked cake design.

VARYING SIZES OF PAINTBRUSHES: for dusting colours, fixing mistakes and painting. I like to have sable ones in 00, 0, 1, 2, 3 and 4.

STENCILS: used for making patterns or pictures on cakes. Use with airbrush machines or to be filled in by hand with edible paints or dusts (see Stencil Cowboy Cake project on page 134).

POLYSTYRENE SEPARATORS: squares or circles of a shallower depth than cake dummies.

POLYSTYRENE DUMMIES: 'fake' cakes.

QUILTING OR STITCHING WHEELS

FRILLING STICKS: small tools with a pointed end that aid frilling of ruffles or flowers.

FOAM PAD OR CEL PAD: these provide a soft surface when frilling petals, making buttons and using plunger cutters. They give you a surface to press against when adding the veining or pattern from a plunger cutter, making impressions on sugar shapes or pressing out waves and curls on paste petals, leaves and buttons.

SILICONE MOULDS AND PUSH MOULDS

IMPRESSION OR EMBOSSING PINS: rolling pins with patterns on them that enable you to make patterns and impressions on sugarpaste directly on the cake, on a decoration or to add imprint patterns to buttercream and royal-iced coverings.

IMPRESSION MATS: you can get a wide variety of patterns, from mock crock to flowers (I use a wood-effect mat in the Stencil Cowboy Cake project on page 134).

FLOPPY MAT: for covering petal paste to prevent it from drying out (you can use a large book wrapped in cling film instead).

CAKE LACE MATS: large mats for creating lace effects.

SUGARCRAFT CUTTERS: metal or plastic plain or plunger-style cutters available in a myriad of shapes and sizes, including blossom, rose, daisy, calyx and leaf cutters.

PACKAGING & TRANSPORTATION:

CAKE BOXES: special boxes available in many sizes to contain cake drums or cards perfectly, and that open out at either side.

CUPCAKE BOXES

CLING FILM

INDIVIDUAL CUPCAKE OR PORTION BOXES

COOKIE BAGS

DO NOT START THE PROJECTS BEFORE READING THIS!

With every project featured in this book, you need to bake the cake sponges before you get started. Bake the sponges at least a day or two in advance so they can cool completely before filling. **Don't rush this stage**. The following day, split, fill and crumb coat as required and chill for a couple of hours in the refrigerator to help them firm up – this makes them easier to decorate. For carved shapes you can chill for longer to make it easier to sculpt.

You can use any cake sponge recipe you like, but for the projects in this book, I have recommended a few of my favourites, which can be found in the **RECIPES** chapter on pages 199–223. In this section you will also find recipes for buttercream, cookie dough, cupcakes, toppings and coverings.

A general cake sponge can be kept chilled in the fridge for up to three days (wrap in cling film to avoid the sponge from drying) and frozen for up to three months. Always double wrap in cling film and pop in a large freezer bag to avoid freezer burn. If you are using a frozen sponge, unwrap and leave to defrost fully before you begin the process of decorating/shaping it.

For the fruit cake recipe it's good to bake it at least a couple of weeks in advance. For cupcakes, ideally cook these freshly then top once cooled. However you can cook a day in advance or, if you wish, you can bake and keep them frozen for up to three months. Make sure these are well wrapped in their tins or packaged in cupcake boxes to prevent any damage to their shape or knocking of the cases.

For cookies you can make these and decorate as soon as cooled, or if you wish to bake in advance – these will keep well for up to eight weeks un-iced, if well wrapped in a food bag. Ideally, as with all food, the fresher, the better!

It is worth noting that most of the projects in this book are made up of two cake sponges sandwiched together to make one cake tier, rather than one cake sponge cut in half. Instructions on how to split, fill and cover your cakes can be found in **THE BASICS** chapter on page 162.

Now you can start your projects!

PROJECTS

*Beautiful creations to delight
your friends & family*

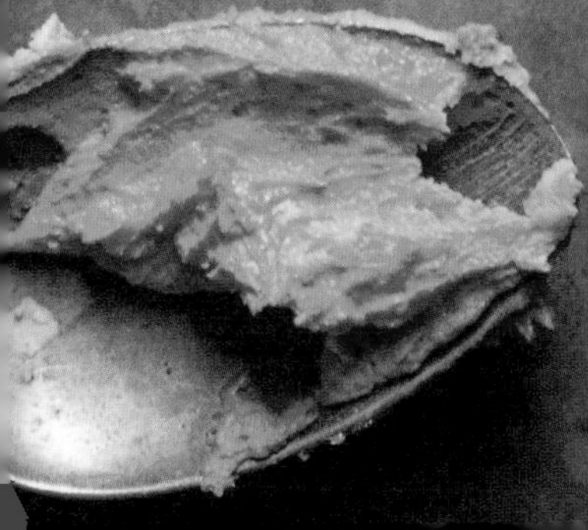

VASE & FLOWERS

I LOVE this one! I got the idea from a photo of a Wedgwood vase with flowers. It's kind of the opposite of the Cupcake Bouquet (see page 33), in which you get the pot as a stand and the 'flowers' are edible; with this cake, the vase is the real cake and the flower posy is fresh flowers! Of course you could use sugar flowers if you wanted to, but I love using real flowers as it makes you think twice... is that REAL? Or cake? I used a photo of a favourite vase to work from, choosing a simple shape so it wouldn't need too much sculpting. This is a perfect celebration cake for a birthday or Mother's Day, or even an unusual wedding centrepiece or table decoration, as an alternative to a regular floral arrangement.

STUFF YOU'LL NEED

Equipment:
› 2 x 12 cm (5 in) round cake drums
› 2 x 10 cm (4 in) round cake drums
› glue stick
› small, sharp knife or ribbon cutter
› bread knife
› pastry brush
› tape measure
› large rolling pin
› guide sticks
› 2 x side smoothers
› 1 x top smoother
› scissors

› scriber needle (optional)
› 2 x small paintbrushes (sable 0/1 for fine lines and 2, 3 or 4 for larger areas)
› piping bag fitted with a No. 2 nozzle
› fresh flowers to arrange after your cake is set up (see 'The Flowers' on page 31)

The Cake:
› 2 x 15 cm (6 in) round cakes (I made deep sponges with 900 g/2 lb Vanilla Bean Sponge (see page 200) in each tin to make a tall base), each filled

with a couple of layers of buttercream of your choice (see pages 216–18)

Ingredients:
› edible glue
› 1.2 kg (2 lb 10 oz) marzipan
› extra buttercream, for sticking
› a little just-boiled apricot jam
› icing (confectioners') sugar, for dusting
› vodka or cooled boiled water
› 1.2 kg (2 lb 10 oz) white sugarpaste
› 150 g (5 oz) white petal paste
› 2 heaped tablespoons soft-peak

royal icing (see page 188 for recipe and consistency guide), dyed with gold paste colour
› dust colours, for painting (I used Sugarflair blossom dusts in dusky pink, aubergine, petal blue, white, navy, rose and light gold lustre)
› rejuvenator spirit
› small glass of water, for brush embroidery

---

01. Start by making the base of the vase shape with two round drums. Glue one of the 12 cm (5 in) cake drums on top of one of the 10 cm (4 in) cake drums, lining the smaller drum up so it's right in the centre of the larger drum, to create a stepped plinth (see 'Construction' on page 28).

02. Take a little sausage of marzipan and fill in the ridge between the cake drums, to start creating the shape of the narrower bottom of the vase. It's easier to create this 'fake' part out of boards at the bottom rather than sponge, and it gives the vase a little more height.

03. Spread a little buttercream on the 12 cm (5 in) cake drum that's stuck on top of the 10 cm (4 in), then pop one of the filled 15 cm (6 in) cakes onto this, positioning it bang in the centre. The sponge will overhang the base, but do not worry – we'll be cutting this down later.

04. Spread a thin layer of buttercream over the top of the sponge, and pop the next filled 15 cm (6 in) cake onto this. Now you have a tall tubular cake on top of the two drums. Place it in the fridge for about an hour to firm up. →

CONSTRUCTION

2 x 15 cm (6 in) sponges – split once

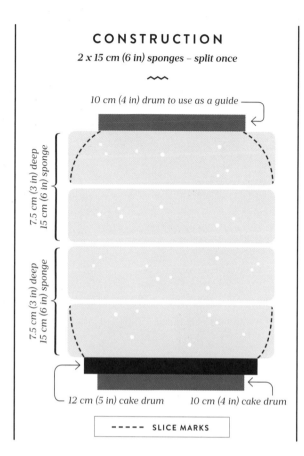

10 cm (4 in) drum to use as a guide

7.5 cm (3 in) deep
15 cm (6 in) sponge

7.5 cm (3 in) deep
15 cm (6 in) sponge

12 cm (5 in) cake drum

10 cm (4 in) cake drum

- - - - - SLICE MARKS

05. Once set, take the sponge out of the fridge. Place the other 10 cm (4 in) cake drum on the top, in the centre of the 15 cm (6 in) cake, and use it as a guide to score around. Use a small, sharp knife to trace a line in the sponge around the drum, so you have a smaller circle scored into the top of the sponge. This is the guide to cut from, to make sure the top of the vase is neat and uniform.

06. Start cutting at an angle from the top of the sponge all around the edge with a bread knife, using the scored line from the 10 cm (4 in) drum as your starting point. Cut the sponge off at a 45-degree angle towards the outside edge of your 'vase', going about

4–5 cm (½–2 in) down the depth. It may help you to measure 5 cm (2 in) down the side from the top and mark this interval so you can make sure it's neat and level. This creates a wedge effect so your vase is narrower at the top. Continue trimming off little pieces of sponge until you are happy with your basic vase shape. You want to create a curved vase top. The softer, rounded look will come when you mould the marzipan and icing layer. Along the bottom edge, carve the base of the 15 cm (6 in) cake in at a slight angle so it looks like the bottom is rounded up from the drum base. Pop it back in the fridge for an hour to firm up again.

07. Remove the vase cake from the fridge and brush the sponge and cake

drums with apricot jam. Measure the height of the cake (mine stood approx. 20 cm/8 in tall). If you are making this design with larger sponges, check the length of marzipan you need to roll out by measuring around the circumference of the vase at the widest point.

TIP › *Wrap a spare length of ribbon around your cake's circumference, then you can snip it and make sure the marzipan is just over this length.*

Dust the work surface with icing sugar and knead then roll out a long strip of marzipan to wrap around your cake (rather than trying to cover the top like a standard shorter cake, as it can tear). I had a 25 cm (10 in) x 56 cm (22 in) strip of marzipan, rolled to guide-stick thickness.

08. Roll the marzipan gently over the rolling pin and lift it up to the cake. Working as quickly as you can, wrap and press the marzipan onto the sides and just over the top edge of the cake. Allow the excess to drape at the back, using your hands to press all over the top and sides, and where the marzipan overlaps at the back, pinch together and use scissors to cut down and remove the excess, leaving you with a rough join (which you can smooth over). Push the marzipan over onto the top of the vase, and press down, trimming away excess creases to leave you with the whole cake roughly covered in a layer of marzipan. Trim off excess marzipan around the base, cutting close to the 10 cm (4 in) drum under the cake. Now, using the top

smoother, press down on the top of the vase shape to make the top flat, and with both side smoothers, work around the cake for a few minutes to smooth and shape, bringing out the angle at the top of the vase, and pushing in over the bottom two drums, to create a narrower bottom and top. Press the smoother onto the cake with strong pressure, particularly at narrower points. Leave to dry overnight.

09. The next day, brush the marzipan 'vase' with vodka or cooled boiled water. Repeat the covering process with the white sugarpaste, wrapping a long tall strip around the cake and trimming the overlapping icing at the back with scissors. Allow the sugarpaste to drop onto the top,

press it over and cut away any creases, so you are left with a flat top. Make sure the icing is completely stuck to the marzipan and trim off any excess around the base of the vase.

10. Smooth over with both side smoothers, to polish and flatten the top, and mould the curved edge of your vase at the top and bottom. Work over the cake for a few minutes to accentuate the flat top and curved sides, using pressure where necessary to bring out the shape. Leave the cake to dry overnight while you make the petal paste 'collar' for the top of the vase. →

11. Knead the petal paste and roll it into a long strip that will be the top of your vase, using guide sticks to ensure an even thickness. You need enough to wrap around the other 10 cm (4 in) cake drum so roll to just over 33 cm (13 in) long and make sure it's wide enough (mine stood 3 cm/1¼ in tall so I rolled it out slightly wider than this). Using a ribbon cutter (this makes it easy to get a super-neat strip), cut along the length of the paste to create the vase collar. If you don't have a ribbon cutter, make a neat strip of card as a guide, along which to cut using a small, sharp knife, to give the collar an even width. Turn the strip onto its side, and wrap around the second 10 cm (4 in) cake drum: this will ensure it sets in a neat circle. Trim off where it overlaps and use edible glue to stick the cut ends together (this will be at the back of the cake so you won't see the join). Leave to set overnight.

12. Firstly, using edible glue, attach the collar to the top of the cake, to create the finished vase. This collar hides the plastic tray for the flower arrangement. Colour roughly 150 g (5 oz) of your white sugarpaste gold with your gold paste. Roll out into a small sausage and wrap it around the bottom of the vase. Use a little edible glue to help it stick, then use your fingers to press it against the base of the vase

to create the gold trim. Trim off any excess then leave to set overnight (see pics 01 and 02 on previous page).

13. Now for the fun part – the decorating. I've used hand painting with edible dust colours for this design, and a free-hand pattern of simple floral shapes. If you find painting by hand a little tricky, use flower cutters and gently trace around the edge of them using a scriber needle to mark out each floral shape or with a light coloured edible pen.

Start by painting light blocks of colour where you need them in rough petal shapes (I used a pale blue to show where the petals are – see picture 03 on previous page). Paint over the edges and details in darker shades, showing the petal and leaf edges and centres, adding shading if you wish. Continue building up the shading and painting over the front and sides of the vase until your flowers are finished. Paint the top collar with your lighter pink shade in a block colour, leave to dry for a short time then, using a very fine brush, paint the pattern around the top (I used clusters of darker pink dots and rough petal shapes coming from these in a repetitive pattern). Pipe a thin pearl trim of gold royal icing around the top of the vase where the collar meets the main cake, to hide the join and add interest (see page 193 for technique).

04

05

06

07

08

~~~~~~~~~~

14. Once you've finished painting, pipe the gold detail
on the design. Add some 'triple dots' on the main cake to
fill white spaces, and pipe around the edges of the petals
of the larger flowers (see pic 04). Use a damp paintbrush to
drag the line of piping towards the centre of the flower, to
create a brush embroidery effect (see pic 05, and page 194
for technique). Leave the icing for a couple of hours, then add
the final details. Make some edible gold paint with gold lustre
and rejuvenator spirit (see pic 06), and paint over the gold
royal iced parts (the pearls, embroidery and gold base trim)
to make the vase shiny and sparkly (see pics 07 and 08). Now
your vase is ready to adorn with fresh flowers. My lovely friend
Lorraine from Shrinking Violet, a local Leigh-on-Sea mum with
an amazing floristry business she runs with the equally talented
Nicky Thain, has given instructions (opposite) for how we made
our arrangement for this design.

THE FLOWERS

~~~

Juliet's cake vase was beautiful and
delicate, and we wanted to replicate this
feel with the choice and style of the flowers.
We prefer to work in a natural, instinctive
way when we make our arrangements and
Juliet had expressed a desire for the flowers
to be loose and flowing; we therefore chose
vibrant and bold flowers that naturally lend
themselves to this style, with some lovely
seasonal garden roses as a main focal point
for the arrangement.

The flowers: white ageratum, blushing bride,
mentha, nigella, lovely rokoko rose, antique
avalanche rose, blueberry rose, piano
garden rose, David Austin Juliet garden rose,
King Arthur garden rose, scabiosa stellata,
trachelium, malus, lisianthus, thlaspi, fern
and asparagus umbellatus.

To make the arrangement for the top of
the vase cake we used wet oasis in a small
9 cm (3½ in) plastic tray.

Firstly, add the foliage or ageratum to form
a loose structure for the height and width of
the arrangement, then gradually add your
larger focal flowers, in our case the garden
roses, followed by smaller flowers, making
sure that the arrangement looks balanced in
terms of size of the flowers and the colours.
Continue to add the remaining flowers and
foliage until the arrangement is full and the
oasis is not visible.

CUPCAKE BOUQUET

I had to include one of these bouquets because they are so stunning, but very simple to make. If you find piping roses with the petal-shaped nozzle tricky, the bouquet still looks amazing using any type of iced cupcake (a simpler swirled topping still looks very flowery when put together in a collection, with piped leaves to finish). I prefer to use meringue buttercream, as it's lighter than regular buttercream, easier to pipe, and not so sweet. These are great for birthday cakes or for gifts for mums, aunties, nans or teachers, or for wedding table decorations – they can then be used as favours so the guests take home a cupcake to munch on the next day, post party! **Makes approximately 20 cupcakes**

STUFF YOU'LL NEED

Equipment:
› a flower pot (mine measured 20 cm/8 in across the top)
› 2 x polystyrene cake dummies
› 12 cm (5 in) polystyrene ball (the polystyrene ball needs to sit within the outside edge of the flower pot)
› large plastic disposable piping bags
› large petal-shaped piping bag nozzles and 1 leaf nozzle (see page 224 for stockists)
› cocktail sticks
› scissors

The Cupcakes:
› 20 baked, un-iced cupcakes (see pages 200–202 for recipe) in white cases, for decorating

Ingredients:
› stiff royal icing, for sticking (see page 188 for recipe and consistency guide, or use shop-bought)
› large handful of sugarpaste
› 20 baked, un-iced cupcakes (see pages 200–202 for recipe) in white cases, for decorating
› approx. 900 g (2 lb) meringue buttercream (see page 221)
in 3 colours (I used dusky pink, peach and white) for the flowers
› approx. 900 g (2 lb) pale green meringue buttercream, for the leaves

01. Start by preparing the pot. You can do this in advance if you like. I've used polystyrene cake dummies, but you could use old polystyrene packaging instead. What you need is a plinth on which to place the polystyrene ball so it appears to poke just over halfway out of the top of your pot. Stick the two cake dummies together with a little royal icing, then stick the ball onto this (using a small ball of sugarpaste and royal icing to help them stick). Squeeze a little royal icing into the bottom of the pot, then pop a piece of sugarpaste, a large handful is enough, into the bottom of the pot (see pics 01 and 02 overleaf). Add a little more royal icing to this and push the polystyrene cake dummies and ball firmly down into the paste (see pic 03 overleaf). Make sure it's standing upright, then leave to dry overnight, or ideally a couple of days, so it sets solid.

02. Fill a piping bag fitted with a petal nozzle with one of the shades of buttercream. Hold the nozzle at a right angle

to one of the cakes (see over page). Start by taking one cake at eye level and holding the nozzle against the cake with the wider fat end touching the sponge and the narrow end pointing upwards. Using gentle pressure, squeeze out some icing onto the middle of the cake's surface, turning the cake as the icing comes out, so that you have a cone-shaped central petal. Stop squeezing and pull the nozzle away (see pics 04–07 overleaf).

TIP › *Practise on a piece of paper a few times so you can see how the buttercream flows out from the nozzle.*

TIP › *Always keep a piece of kitchen paper handy to wipe the nozzle with if you get a build up of buttercream on it.*

03. Continue piping in the same direction, keeping the wide point of the nozzle against the sponge and squeezing →

Hold the nozzle at a right angle to the cupcake

out small lengths of buttercream. With the nozzle's thin tip facing upwards and slightly directed outwards, pipe petals from the centre to the outside of the cupcake edge, in a wrapping motion, as you turn the cake, layering petal-effect lengths of buttercream. Keep turning the cake, building up petals, wrapped around the central bud. Each time you place the nozzle back on the cake, start at the end of the previous petal, to create the overlapping petal effect. Continue until the entire surface of the cupcake is covered. It takes a little practice, but after a few tries you will get the feel for it. Pipe buttercream onto all of the cupcakes in different shades, using clean piping bags and nozzles for each different colour. Pop them in the fridge to chill for 30 minutes.

~~~~~~~

04. Now for assembling the bouquet. Push a cocktail stick into the polystyrene ball (this stops the cupcakes from

falling off). Push them around the bottom first, so that the first row of cupcakes can rest against the edge of the pot. Take a cupcake and pipe a small dab of royal icing on its bottom to stick the cupcake to the ball (see pic 08). Push the cupcake, base first, onto the cocktail stick until the base and royal icing squishes onto the ball (see pic 09). Now go all around the bottom edge to create a row. Butt them up closely together so that the gaps for the buttercream leaves aren't too large.

~~~~~~~

05. Continue, working around the ball and upwards, covering the whole ball with cupcakes. The cupcakes below will support the cupcakes above. If you end up with a slightly larger gap that you can't fit your last cake in, make this the back of your display and just fill it with extra leaves.

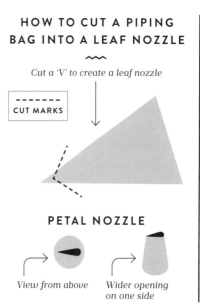

06. Fill a large piping bag fitted with a large leaf nozzle, or simply cut with a 'V' at the end (see diagram opposite) to create the leafy effect, with green buttercream. Pipe leaves by pointing the nozzle in the gaps between the cupcake 'flowers', against the ball, and pipe ruffled leaves from the inside outwards against the sides of the cake cases (see pic 10). Use a strong pressure, then release the pressure and pull away to create a pointed end where the nozzle or piping bag has pulled the buttercream into a peak at the tip of the leaf. Fill all of the gaps until the design is full and finished.

TIP › *Buttercream holds its shape well at room temperature, but if the weather is very warm, you may need to chill the bouquet until you want to display it. Ideally the cakes should be at room temperature when you eat them. I would not recommend making this and transporting it to a venue when assembled: instead, take the cupcakes and leaf buttercream along separately and pop them in on-site. It doesn't take long and saves the headache of driving at 5 miles an hour with the fear of it tumbling – it is fairly top-heavy!*

HOW TO CUT A PIPING BAG INTO A LEAF NOZZLE

Cut a 'V' to create a leaf nozzle

CUT MARKS

PETAL NOZZLE

View from above

Wider opening on one side

TATTOOED SAILOR NAUTICAL COOKIE EXPLOSION

I love using cookies as cake decorations in the bakery. We made a showbiz cake for Dizzee Rascal with stars and edible image cookies. You can adapt the colour scheme, of course, or use any shape of cookie. Using cookies on sticks is also a fun way to add an explosion detail and give your cake more height and a bit of wow factor. If your cake-covering skills aren't perfect, you don't need to worry because you can strategically place your cookies over any lumpy bumpy bits! I made the roses with modelling chocolate (which tastes better than sugarpaste, has a lovely sheen, and doesn't dry out and crack), creating a two-tone rose, but make them all in one shade if you prefer. You can make them weeks in advance, leaving them on a cake board wrapped in cling film in a cake box until ready to use. Make the chocolate roses and ice the cookies, including the piping detail, at least a day before you want to assemble the cake, so it's easier to handle.

STUFF YOU'LL NEED

Equipment:
› plastic document wallet
› small, sharp knife
› spare cake drum, for drying
› small plastic rolling pin
› ribbon cutter
› piping bag with a No. 2 nozzle
› guide sticks
› turntable
› paintbrush
› cake smoother
› length of 1.5 cm (½ in) wide black ribbon
› cocktail sticks

The Cakes:
› 23 cm (9 in) round cake (any flavour you wish), split, filled, crumb-coated and iced in white sugarpaste
› 15 cm (6 in) round cake, split, filled, crumb-coated and iced in navy sugarpaste on a 30 cm (12 in) round drum iced in navy sugarpaste (see pages 182–85)

Ingredients:
› decorated and royal-iced flooded heart-shaped vanilla cookies in different sizes and colours, with some on sticks for the top of the cake (see page 213 for cookies recipe, page 227 for cookie templates and page 122 for icing techniques)
› 400 g (14 oz) modelling chocolate, in 2 shades of red for the vintage roses (I used Christmas red, dyeing a quarter of this red with a little dark-brown paste to make a duller red). You'll need approx. 25 g (1 oz) to make 1 rose – once trimmed, a small rose will weigh about 10 g (⅓ oz), a medium rose 15 g (½ oz) and a large rose about 25 g (1 oz)
› 50 g (2 oz) petal paste
› stiff royal icing, for sticking
› 2 heaped tablespoons black soft-peak royal icing (see page 188 for recipe and consistency guide)
› approx. 500 g (1 lb 2 oz) each of black and white sugarpaste for the stripes
› small cup of boiled water
› icing (confectioners') sugar, for dusting

01. Cut open the document wallet along the outer edge and bottom so that you can open it up like a book.

02. First, make all of the roses. Roll out some of the dull red and bright red modelling chocolate into two sausages, about 1.5 cm (¾ in) thick. Cut the sausages into 1 cm (½ in) chunks with a small, sharp knife (see pic 01 overleaf).

03. Lay the document wallet open on the work surface and line up the chocolate chunks in rows on one side of the open wallet (this prevents pieces sticking to your hands or the work surface). Make about 4–5 rows of four pieces across, leaving space between each one (see pic 02 overleaf). →

04. Close the wallet over the chocolate chunks and, with the base of your thumb (just above your wrist), push down on each chunk to flatten it out (see pic 03).

~~~~~~~

05. Gently run the tip of your thumb along the petal edge nearest the seam, to thin it out (don't make it too thin – all you need is to pinch off the very edge). Repeat with all the petals.

~~~~~~~

06. Carefully peel off the top of the wallet and pick up one darker red petal by its fat base. You will notice that as you lift it from the wallet, it naturally curls one way. Make sure that the curved edge is facing towards you as you work with

it. For the centre of the rose, gently tuck in the petal at one edge and roll into a tight cone (see pic 04).

~~~~~~~

07. Now take a second dark red petal off the wallet, making sure it's curling away from the rose's centre and attach it to the first central petal, making sure that the second petal is a couple of millimetres higher than the first one. This will ensure that the middle part doesn't stick up above the outer petals (what we in the biz call 'trumpeting'). Wrap petal number two around the first one, gently pressing your fingers on the base to attach it. Only handle the fat base of the petal – the top thin part is easily damaged (see pic 05).

08. Continue adding further petals, this time in the brighter red, in the same manner: overlapping the previous petal and making sure each petal you add is a little higher up than the previous one, until you have a uniform circular rose (you'll probably need 6–8 petals per flower, see pic 06). You can make them different sizes: three petals will give you a rose bud, more petals (up to 12) create a larger, open rose. This cake design looks lovely using a few sizes.

09. Gently pinch each petal at the edge to create a little movement (see pic 07). This adds a delicate touch and makes the flowers look more real. Roll the base of the flower between your fingers to make sure it's completely stuck and, using a sharp knife, gently cut away the excess chocolate (this can be wrapped and re-used) to make the rose flat at the base. Place on a spare cake drum. Make as many as you need for your cake; I used about 30 in various sizes. →

10. Roll out the petal paste to create a scroll for the name on your cookie. Roll it fairly thinly (about 2 mm) and cut a 4 cm- (1½ in-) wide strip with a ribbon cutter or knife (see pic 08). Using a sharp knife, cut a 'V' shape at either end to create a ribbon effect (see pic 09). Dab or pipe a little white royal icing on the cookie where you wish to place the scroll (see pic 10). Pick up the scroll and bend it at one end to create a wave at the end on one side, tucking under some of the length as shown in pic 11. Press down at the point where you want to loop the scroll back across the cookie, and finish off the other side in the same way (see pic 12). Leave it to set for a few hours (or make it a few days in advance). Pipe your name or message over it once it has set using your black soft-peak royal icing (see pic 13).

~~~~~~~~

11. The day before you assemble the cake, add details to your cookies and some 'snail trail' piping (see page 193 for technique) around the edges, or dots to add detail around some of the borders of the heart cookies. Leave them to dry before attaching them to the cake (see pic 14).

~~~~~~~~

12. Make stripes for the base cake by rolling out the black and white sugarpaste to guide-stick thickness (see pic 15) and cutting long strips to wrap around the cake (for the 23 cm/9 in round base cake you'll need each strip to be about 90 cm/35 in long). Always roll sugarpaste strips out a little longer than you need, so that you get a neat join at the back. Measure the height of your base cake to work out where you want the stripes to finish (just below the top where the cake's edge begins to curve) and divide this by six. (For mine, 9 cm/3½ in depth meant that I needed six strips, each 1.5 cm/¾ in thick.) Use a ribbon cutter or a strip of card and a sharp knife to make strips (see pic 16 overleaf), cutting six strips in total (three black, three white). →

14

15

13. Place your two-tiered cake on the turntable. Brush a little water around the bottom of the base tier, running along the edge of the cake board (see pic 17). Roll one of the lengths of sugarpaste up onto the rolling pin and place the coiled piece of sugarpaste up against the cake, resting on the iced board (see pic 18). Starting at the back, unroll the strip of sugarpaste and press it gently onto the cake (see pic 19). Go over the sugarpaste with a cake smoother. Take a sharp knife and cut over both ends to create a neat join at the back. Repeat this process with a black stripe, wrapping it around the cake directly above the white one and continue until the cake is covered in stripes.

14. Cover the bottom of the top tier, where it meets the base tier, with a length of black ribbon to hide the join, securing the ribbon with a dab of royal icing (see pic 20).

15. Finally, add your cookie decorations, placing them where you like, making sure your message or name is at the front (see pic 21). Use stiff white royal icing to attach the cookies.

TIP › *If larger cookies feel like they may slip or fall out of place, push in cocktail sticks to keep them in place while the icing sets overnight, then simply remove them the next day.*

Push the cookies on sticks into the top of the cake (see pic 22), trimming the sticks down a little if necessary with sharp scissors or wire cutters. Add the roses to the cake wherever you wish, dabbing a little stiff white royal icing to the underside of each rose as edible glue, though taking care not to use too much (you don't want it to show at the front of the flower). Round of applause – you're done!

TOP TIP
~~~

Remember to choose
the best side of the
cake first: all cakes
have a back and will
look better from a
certain angle, no
matter how great
you are at covering!

MONOCHROME CHEVRON CAKE

This has to be one of my favourite projects. I got the idea for this cake when I met my lovely publisher, Kate, for the first time. She's got wicked style and was wearing an amazing Marni necklace, and I couldn't stop thinking about the eye-catching and colourful design. That night I had an idea of how to create a cake that would bring the necklace to life, and I'm bloomin' happy with this one! What I love about it is that the structural chocolate plastic-style flowers are completely edible, with no wires. Also, because they're lacquered, they look just like costume jewellery (and Kate's necklace). You could use any colours, of course, or a metallic spray. I made a version with gold chevrons for Fortnum and Mason, using a caramel-colour petal paste, painted with gold lustre. The possibilities for this cool, sleek design are endless. It is a pretty straightforward project once you get the hang of the chevrons – just take your time. The paper transfer technique makes it easy to get straight, geometric patterns that look sharp and neat onto a cake.

STUFF YOU'LL NEED

Equipment:
› length of 1 cm- (½ in-) wide white ribbon
› small rolling pin
› 5–6 plastic petal-shaped cutters in 3 different sizes, or card templates to cut around
› modelling tool
› silver foil (optional)
› ruler or tape measure
› chevron template (see template on page 49)
› card

› pencil
› baking parchment
› scissors
› scalpel
› paintbrush
› side smoother
› cocktail sticks

The Cakes:
› 23 cm (9 in) and 15 cm (6 in) square cakes (any flavour you wish) split, filled and iced in white sugarpaste, stacked on

a 33 cm (13 in) square cake drum iced in white sugarpaste (see pages 182–85)

Ingredients:
› icing (confectioners') sugar, for dusting
› modelling chocolate in 3 colours (I used approx. 300 g/10½ oz each of red, tangerine and claret Cocoform)
› edible food lacquer (optional – see page 224 for stockists)

› Trex vegetable fat
› 200 g (7 oz) black petal paste
› edible glue
› stiff-peak royal icing, for sticking
› handful of white sugarpaste, for sticking

01. Wrap and fix the white ribbon to the bottom of the top cake tier (see pic 01 overleaf).

02. Next, make your chocolate flowers (at least a day in advance, so they can dry out and firm up). Dust the work surface with icing sugar and roll out the modelling chocolate no thinner than 3 mm. Cut out several petal shapes in different sizes and colours. For the large flowers cut out three petal sizes; for smaller ones just use a small and medium petal (see pic 02 overleaf). I made nine flowers for this cake.

03. Fold each chocolate petal shape in half (don't press so hard that they stick) and open it back out, then fold it in the opposite direction, so you've divided it into four parts. Take the largest petal shape and pinch it together in the centre, then use your fingers to open out the shape into a cupped circle. This will hold a smaller flower (see pic 03 overleaf). Pinch the smaller petal shape in the same way, opening it back out. Now nest the smaller folded petal in the larger one (see pic 04 overleaf). Use a modelling tool to push the centre of the small one against the centre of the larger. Repeat with the smallest shape. Make as many flowers as you like and leave them on their sides to set. →

04. Once the chocolate flowers are set, spray them with edible food lacquer if you like, or use any edible shine spray or edible varnish (see pic 05). Leave to dry, and store until ready to use. You can make them a few weeks in advance, but allow at least 24 hours for them to set. The spray takes a couple of hours to dry properly.

05. Make the chevron template once your cake is iced (cake sizes vary once the sponge is covered with marzipan and icing). Choose the best side of the cake to be the front and measure its height and width. Make sure the chevron pattern is at least three rows – I think odd numbers look better – and make sure the points of the top chevron just protrudes over the top edge of your cake. Measure and take into account the width of the ribbon (see pic 06). Scan the chevron pattern on your computer, adjusting the height and width as necessary, and print twice onto card (or paper, to stick to card after), or hand-draw the zig-zag chevron pattern neatly, twice, using a ruler. You need the ends of the chevron strips both pointing up or both pointing down, so that the corners will match up to the side next to it.

06. Once your two templates are ready, use one copy to trace over: place baking parchment over the template and neatly trace the three chevron strips (see pic 07).

TIP › *Line up the baking parchment carefully to match the straight edge of the template, so that you can easily transfer the pattern to the cake.*

07. Cut one chevron strip off the other chevron template. This is what you'll use to cut around on the petal paste. Using your fingertip, rub a little Trex over the chevron pattern on the baking parchment. This will hold the petal paste chevron strip on securely when you lift it, but won't stick the chevrons to the parchment (see pic 08).

08. Have your edible glue, or thinned out royal icing, and Trex to hand before starting to roll out the petal paste as it dries out quickly. Knead the petal paste, then dust the work surface with a little icing sugar; take care not to get too much icing sugar on the top of the paste: we want sleek perfection here, not a powdery finish. Roll out 50 g (2 oz) at a time – enough to cover the whole template – until it's really thin and, working quickly so it doesn't dry out, cut out three chevron strips with your scalpel (see pic 09 overleaf).

09. Place the three strips onto your Trex-covered baking parchment template, lining them up as neatly as possible over the traced lines. Brush the chevrons with edible glue (see pics 10 and 11 overleaf). Carefully lift your pattern up and hold it against the front of your cake (see pic 12 overleaf). Work from the top tier of the cake down, $\longrightarrow$

01

05

If you find they are not holding their shape, make little wells out of silver foil, to hold them in their cupped shape while they set. If it's really hot, pop them in the fridge. Once set, they will keep their shape at room temperature.

so that you don't knock any chevrons below. Check it is running straight along the top edge of the ribbon and, once you are sure it is straight, gently press the pattern against the cake using a side smoother (see pic 13). Peel away the paper, to reveal the perfectly straight chevron pattern on your cake (see pic 14). If there's any Trex build-up on the chevrons, just rub it in gently with your finger or a cloth (it will give the chevrons a nice polished look). Repeat on all sides of the cake, lining up the corners to the front chevrons as neatly as you can with your fingers. Petal paste has a little give, so if you need to bend it slightly, you can. Repeat this for the bottom tier of the cake. Once your cake is covered with the chevron pattern, leave it to set overnight.

TIP › *If you do find you have a powdery finish on your chevrons, dust off with a dry pastry brush or add a tiny bit of Trex to the tip of your finger and gently rub any spots away once the chevrons have set.*

TIP › *I always decorate the front first, so that it is the most perfectly covered bit, then you can work up against this from the sides, leaving the back until last (this is where you might get a small gap, which won't matter as it will be the back of the cake).*

10. Finally, stick the chocolate flowers onto the cake, using a little stiff white royal icing and placing them wherever you like. Use the extra handful of white sugarpaste, rolled into a lump (smaller than the flowers, so you can't see it), to lean the top flowers up against, arranging the flowers around the paste. Add a cocktail stick if necessary, to support the chocolate flowers until they set (see pic 15).

And there you have it. A cool, chic, monochrome cake fit for the modern bride or party gal!

09

10

11

12

13

14

15

TOP TIP

~~~

If you have dodgy corner joins, just cover them with a chocolate decoration and no one will ever know!

CHEVRON TEMPLATE

FRAMED INSECT TAXIDERMY

*I think this is my favourite project in the book. It was inspired by a recent birthday, when I was given some beautiful framed butterflies and a cicada as presents from friends and family. I know some people don't like the idea of these, but for those who do, these delicious edible bugs are SO cool, as they almost look real! I had the idea for the design in a dream, and woke up just knowing they would look amazing. Although they look elaborate, they are pretty straightforward to make. As long as you try to keep each insect wing or side as near a mirror image to the opposite one, they look fab. The heroes of the design are the fantastic edible metallic pens and paints. They are fun to work with and pretty forgiving if you have a caketastrophe. I've used several colours, but if you don't have many, adapt some of the designs and just use paste colours with water. **Makes 9 cake cubes***

STUFF YOU'LL NEED

Equipment:
› photos of butterflies or bugs
› wing templates (I stuck pictures onto card and cut them out – see templates on page 226)
› rolling pin
› scalpel
› modelling tools (I used a blade and shell tool, tiny ball tool, Dresden tool and a pointed scriber tool)
› small paintbrush
› cocktail sticks
› 7.5 cm (3 in) square card template

› bread knife
› guide sticks
› sharp knife
› 2 x side smoothers
› spare cake board
› piping bag with a No. 2 nozzle

The Cake:
› 23 cm (9 in) square Vanilla Bean Sponge cake (see pages 200–202)

Ingredients:
› icing (confectioners') sugar, for dusting
› 50 g (2 oz) white petal paste

› 50 g (2 oz) white Cocoform modelling chocolate (see page 224 for stockists), for bug bodies
› edible metallic paints in pen form and in pots (I used Rainbow Dust pens and pots – see stockists on page 224)
› a little just-boiled apricot jam
› 600 g (1 lb 5 oz) marzipan
› vodka or cooled boiled water
› 700 g (1 lb 9 oz) white sugarpaste
› 500 g (1 lb 2 oz) brown modelling paste (white paste marbled with black, chestnut,

caramel, dark brown and bronze paste colours), for the frames
› edible glue
› a few black stamens with the beads cut off, for antennae (optional)
› a little sugarpaste, for sticking
› 2 tablespoons black stiff-peak royal icing (see page 188 for recipe and consistency guide, or use shop-bought)

01. Make the bug bodies and wings in advance – a few weeks ahead is fine, using the photos to guide you with the body shapes. I made a few wingless beetles, a couple of winged beetles, cicada-style, and some butterflies. Make wings by rolling out the petal paste to the thickness of a lasagne sheet or even thinner. Use a scalpel to cut out several pairs of wings in different shapes (see pic 01 overleaf); I've got butterfly and beetle ones here. Leave them to dry and set overnight. Make bodies by moulding small pieces of Cocoform for the large beetles and petal paste for the tiny butterfly bodies. Mould them into little sausages or small

cones, depending on the shape of the bug's body. The butterfly body shape is a tiny cone, the beetles start from a larger sausage shape. They don't need to be exact, but bear in mind that you want your finished bug to fit in the edible frame, so for your butterflies make sure the pair of wings and body will fit comfortably within it. Mark out the impression of the central beetle shells and their large buggy eyes with a Dresden tool or pointed scriber tool. Use modelling tools to make shapes to define the thorax, head or beetly armour, (see pic 02 overleaf). Leave the wings and bodies to dry. →

01

02

03

02. Now for the fun part – painting the detail with metallic paints. For the bodies of the larger beetles I used different shades of metallic blues, greens, and green and copper (see pic 03). On one of my butterfly wing pairs I used a bright metallic blue, and painted a thick black line over the outer edge of the wing. To add fine detail I used a dragging motion from the edge of the wing towards the middle with the end of a cocktail stick, then mirrored the detail on the other wing (see pic 04). For the very bright butterfly I used a pale green metallic and added splodges of bronze, gold and blue, then some black. I dragged the black throughout the wings. You can use any pattern, as long as you mirror it on the opposite wing (make a few spares in case of breakages). Leave all the body and wing components to dry.

03. Use the card template to cut out the cubes of cake by cutting out three lengths one way, then turning the cake round and cutting across the three lengths to make nine cubes. Transfer to the fridge to chill.

04. Brush the cakes with the boiled apricot jam.

05. Lightly dust the work surface with icing sugar, then roll out the marzipan to a large square using guide sticks. Roll again without the guide sticks to make the marzipan slightly thinner. Cut out squares of marzipan large enough to cover the tops and sides of your cube cakes.

TIP › *See pictures 02–04 on page 90 for the 'World's Best Dad' Chocolate Mini Bites – the round cakes are covered in marzipan in the same way these cubed cakes are.*

06. Place each piece of marzipan over the cakes and gently smooth over. Using side smoothers, push the marzipan against the sides of the cakes, pressing firmly to make the cakes square. Keep pushing against the surface with the smoothers to give you a line along which to cut away the excess. Use a sharp knife to cut away the excess marzipan and re-roll it if you need to. Leave to dry for a few hours or overnight before icing. →

04

TOP TIP

Try and make the wing patterns symmetrical for a realistic look

05

06

07

07. Brush the marzipan with vodka or cooled boiled water and repeat steps 5 and 6 with the white sugarpaste (see pic 05). Try to get the cakes as neat and square as you can. Leave to dry overnight.

08. Now, add the frame detail. For a marbled wood effect, knead three brown shades into white modelling paste but don't knead it fully – allow for some streaks, which will create the marbled effect. For black or bronze frames, use liquorice paste colour or caramel. Roll out your coloured paste to guide-stick thickness and, using the guide sticks as a frame maker, press them gently into the paste. This makes an indentation on each side of the paste strip which will be a guide for the width. Cut several strips: you'll need them to be slightly longer than the 7.5 cm (3 in) cube sides (see pic 08).

09. Brush edible glue along the outside top edge of the square cake. Begin by laying one strip along one edge, keeping it straight. Leave the excess hanging over the side. Lay the next strip on the following side, overlapping the previous strip, so that then you can cut in over the two pieces at a 45-degree angle, to create a neat diagonal join. Pull out the excess and neatly pinch the cut corners together to create the sharp corner of the frame (see pic 07). Continue in the same manner until you have four strips all cut to create

a frame. Repeat with all of the cakes. If you want to make the frames shiny, brush them with a little food varnish or, for a bronze effect, use a metallic paint pen or paint and brush.

10. It's time to bring the creations to life! If you are using stamens for antennae, use a pin tool to make a hole in the front of the body, then push the stamen into the body (trimming them down if necessary). Curl them slightly outward. (If you want the decorations to be 100 per cent edible, leave the stamens off.) Use a tiny ball of sugarpaste just slightly smaller than the body, a few millimetres high, to elevate the insect body from the cake. If you are adding wings, place a small amount of white sugarpaste, again smaller than the wing so you can't see it from above, and shape it into a little wedge to set the wings so they are standing slightly upright. Place the wings right up against the body. For wingless bugs just leave the body on and pipe their little sugar legs: pipe royal icing against the side of the bug where you think the leg would protrude from, using a gentle pressure and pulling outwards in the direction of where you want to place the foot (see pic 08). Use a stronger pressure to make this foot part a bit fatter, or add another spindly small piped line to create more detail. When the legs have dried completely, paint over parts of these with gold or bronze if you like, to make them appear more realistic. Display in a group, or box as a freaky cakey gift!

NOTE

~~~

These cakes are small, so you don't want a very thick coating of marzipan or sugarpaste that overpowers the cake.

OLD-SCHOOL TRAINER

This is one cool project – a perfect cake for a man (or of course a lady, but we always find it's more difficult to come up with cake designs for blokes). It takes patience, but is well worth the effort. You can make it in any colour to personalise it for whoever you are making it for. Do work with a real shoe, and measure its height and length, as it is tricky to get the details right if you just work from pictures. You could use edible print such as leopard print on some of the stripes – the world is your oyster when it comes to colour and detail. I've stuck to an old-school white box-fresh look! You can scale the cake up or down. I made my shoe the same size as one I'd wear (size 3/US 5!), starting with a 23 cm (9 in) square sponge. If you are making a bigger or smaller cake, measure the sole of your shoe, then pick the right size tin. Bake a deep sponge, or a few sponges to sandwich together, so you can be sure your shoe cake will be high enough.

STUFF YOU'LL NEED

Equipment:
> bread knife or serrated palette knife
> card sole template (see page 228)
> tape measure
> edible-ink pen
> guide sticks
> large rolling pin
> pastry brush
> cake smoother
> pin tool or scriber needle
> length of ribbon, twice as long as your shoe
> scalpel
> kitchen paper or cling film
> stitching wheel tool
> small polka-dot cutter or straw
> ribbon cutter

The Cake
> Vanilla Bean Sponge cake (see pages 200–202) I used 2 kg (4 lb 6 oz) batter to fill a 23 cm (9 in) square tin), split 3 times and filled with buttercream

Ingredients:
> 1 kg (2 lb 3 oz) marzipan
> icing (confectioners') sugar, for dusting
> a little just-boiled apricot jam
> vodka or cooled boiled water
> 1.25 kg (2 lb 12 oz) white sugarpaste
> approx. 200 g (7 oz) orange/rust modelling paste (I used Renshaw tangerine/apricot paste and chestnut paste colour for the middle inner part of the shoe and tongue underside)
> 200 g (7 oz) white modelling paste, for white detail on the side of the shoe, the bottom sole trim, laces and front of the shoe
> approx. 200 g (7 oz) blue/green modelling paste, coloured with baby blue and mint green paste colour for the front decorative stripe, lace hole detail and back detail

01. Cut the split and filled sponge to a rough rectangle just bigger then the sole you are working from, and tall enough to reach the height of the back of your shoe. Chill the sponge block for a couple of hours (this will make it much easier to carve without crumbling or breaking).

02. Once set firm, place the sole template on top of the block of sponge, and cut the sponge out to the shape of the sole.

03. Begin roughly carving out the shoe shape with a bread knife (see pic 01 overleaf). If you work slowly you may find that the sponge becomes too soft, and you need to stop and re-chill it. Measure the shoe you are copying in increments, and mark each increment with an edible-ink pen on the sponge (mark the middle of the shoe where the laces end, the toe of the shoe, and when the angle begins to slope down from the back of the shoe). Keep cutting away until a wedge shape begins to form.

04. Sculpt the rounded top edge of the shoe by eye, making a small indentation with the knife where the foot hole begins to sink in (don't hollow it out far). This takes patience – keep checking proportions, bending down so that the →

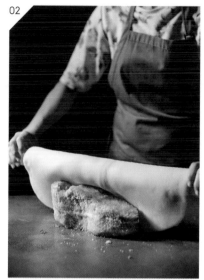

cake is at eye level to check the real shoe shape against your piece of sponge. Finally, cut a small channel down the front where the lace detail will go. Chill the shaped sponge again, for at least an hour, to firm up.

〜〜〜

05. Knead the marzipan to soften it, then dust the work surface with icing sugar and roll out the marzipan to guide-stick thickness, in a strip big enough to cover the whole length of the shoe and wrap over the sides too. Brush the sponge all over with the hot apricot jam then, using your rolling pin, lift the piece of marzipan up and lay it over onto the sponge (see pic 02). Using your fingers, press the marzipan onto the trainer and down over the sides. Push it onto the sponge to start bringing out the curved lines and contours, then use a smoother to bring out the details (see pic 03). Use the end of your rolling pin to push in a little where the 'foot' will go and smooth out the indentation on the channel where the tongue and laces will fit (see pic 04). Trim off the excess marzipan from the base around the edge of the sole. Leave to dry and set overnight.

〜〜〜

06. Brush the whole marzipan trainer with vodka or cooled boiled water to make the surface tacky (see pic 05). Repeat the covering process with the white sugarpaste, using the end of the rolling pin again to push in a little where

04

05

06

07

08

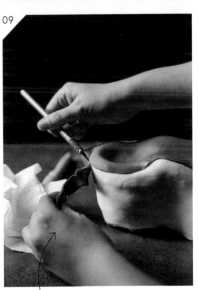

09

the 'foot' goes in (see pics 06 and 07). If you notice any air bubbles in the sugarpaste, pop them with a pin tool or scriber needle and smooth out the air. Leave to dry and set overnight.

07. Now, add the detail. Begin by rolling out the rust-coloured piece of modelling paste for the top of the shoe to show the top, back edge and inner detail. Use the tape measure or a bit of ribbon to give you the length you

need to roll out to, making it just a bit larger than you need. Roll it out to a very thin strip, then dampen the trainer just where the 'foot' dip is, and place the piece of paste on top (see pic 08). Push it into the shoe and gently lay over the edge. Using a scalpel, carefully cut around the shape, neatening it up, and trim off where the laces will hide (see pic 09). Once you are happy with the shape, smooth over the cut edge with your fingers, to join the colour to the white base. →

TOP TIP

~~~

With the sugarpaste details, don't try to cut out the precise shape on the work surface; do the final cutting actually on the shoe itself, tailoring each piece to fit with a scalpel to give the shoe a neater, cleaner finish.

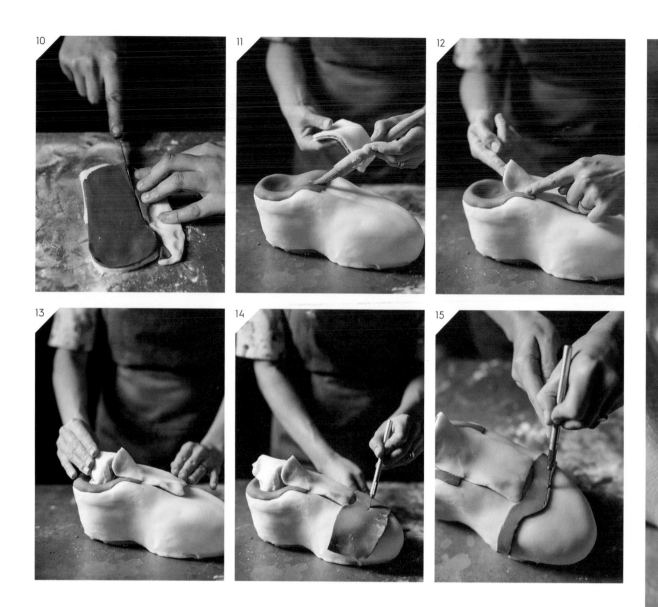

08. Add the tongue detail. I used two colours of modelling paste here: white and rust. Roll out both pieces thinly on a surface lightly dusted with icing sugar, to be just a bit longer and wider than you need, then brush the top of the white piece with vodka or cooled boiled water and lay the rust piece over the top. Cut out the rough shape of the tongue (see pic 10). Brush the shoe with a little vodka or cooled boiled water where you are going to attach your tongue, and place it onto the shoe (see pics 11 and 12). If the shape isn't quite right, trim it until you are happy with it. Leave the tongue part poking up and use a little scrunched up kitchen paper to make a support for it so it can hold its shape while setting (see pic 13).

09. Continue adding the trainer details. Look at the patterns and place the pieces on the shoe cake in the order that they have been stitched onto the shoe. I placed the main front detail next (see pic 14). You need to apply all of these thin pieces first, adding the outer sole trim and front detail at the end. To create the sewn/stitched effect of some of the coloured fabric, use a stitching wheel tool or make little dashes with the end of your scalpel (see pic 15). Cut the lace holes on the side panels using a small polka-dot cutter or the end of a straw, once the panels are on but not stuck. Use your fingertips behind the panel and cut against these in the place where you want to punch out the holes.

10. Once all of the main details are placed, including eyelets for the laces at the top, finish off the detail with sugary laces. Use a ribbon cutter to cut a long strip of modelling paste for these, so that you can keep the movement showing (the modelling paste holds its shape well). Cut out the small lengths on the top where the laces go. Use the end of your scalpel or a similar modelling tool to 'tuck' the modelling paste down into the hole so it appears that these laces are threaded through the holes. Finally, add longer lengths of lace to the top eyelets and allow to trail down over the shoe. Pinch the end of each lace with your fingers to create the end detail (see pic 16). Leave to set overnight before transporting, lifting or displaying.

LYDIA'S LOVEHEART COOKIES

These cute cookies are perfect for parties, presents or to make with friends. In Fancy Nancy it's very much a family affair, and Lydia, our middle child, has been working at the bakery since she was about 13. She is brilliant at art and makes all kinds of cakes, so I wanted her to suggest a design for this book. I'll hand you over to Lydia: 'I'm Juliet's eldest daughter, Lydia, and I really enjoy baking (I have a part-time job in Mum's cake shop). It was my sister Ruby's birthday and I wanted to make some cookies for her to give out to her friends, so I thought that personalising them would be a cool idea. To appeal to everyone, I made these simple loveheart cookies in different colours. They're great for party bags or gifts: put them in bags and tie them with ribbon.' **Makes about 20 cookies**

STUFF YOU'LL NEED

Equipment:
› rolling pin
› guide sticks
› round cutter, the same size that you used to cut out your cookie dough; we used a 10 cm (4 in) one to allow plenty of space for the heart and name within (or use the round template on page 227 to make a round piece of card to cut around)
› piping bag with the end snipped off

› cake smoother
› heart-shaped cutter, slightly smaller than the round cutter (or a heart-shaped piece of card, see page 227 for template)
› piping bag with a No. 2 nozzle

The Cookies:
› round cookies (we used 1 quantity of basic Vanilla Cookie dough, see pages 213–14)

Ingredients:
› icing (confectioners') sugar, for dusting
› sugarpaste in pastel candy colours: you need about 30 g (1 oz) per cookie in this size so make up equal amounts of pink, mint green, lemon and cream. (Lydia used Renshaw ready-to-roll colours in green, yellow, pink and ivory but you could make up pastel shades with paste colours if you prefer,

with a little claret, mint green and egg yellow)
› a little soft-peak royal icing in white
› 2 tablespoons soft-peak royal icing, coloured with paste colour (Lydia used ruby and claret to make a deep raspberry red shade for the heart and name writing – see page 188 for recipe and consistency guide, or use shop-bought)

01. Lightly dust the work surface with icing sugar and roll out all of your sugarpaste colours to guide-stick thickness, then remove the guide sticks and continue rolling them a little thinner, to a thickness of 2–3 mm.

02. Cut out all of your sugar circles with the round cutter.

03. Lay out the cookies on the work surface and pipe a drizzle of white royal icing over each one using a piping bag with the end snipped off (see pic 01 overleaf).

04. Lift the sugar circles and pop them all onto the cookies, making sure they're central (see pic 02 overleaf). Once you've got them all on, gently press each one to stick it down and flatten it neatly onto the cookie with your cake smoother.

05. With the heart cutter, make an impression by gently pushing the heart into the circle. This will give you a perfect guideline for piping a neat heart (see pic 03 overleaf).

06. Personalise all of your cookies with the coloured royal icing in a piping bag with a No. 2 nozzle fitted, piping your friends' or family's names on in any writing style you like. →

01

02

03

Then, starting at the top in the middle, with gentle pressure, begin piping the royal icing over the heart guideline (see pic 04). Do this slowly, lifting the piping bag slightly above the cookie and allowing the line to drop down slowly using gravity. This will make your line neat and less wobbly. Once you reach the bottom point, stop squeezing the bag and gently touch the nozzle into the heart at the surface and pull the bag away. Repeat from the top down again along the other side of the heart shape.

~~~~~~~~~~

07. Leave the cookies to dry for at least 12 hours, then give them out to guests, plate up a display at your party, or pop them into individual bags and tie with some ribbon to make the perfect party favour.

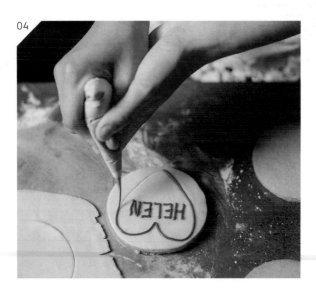

04

TOP TIP

〜

If you aren't confident at piping lettering, you can buy little letter stampers in craft shops or online (see page 224 for stockists) and press out the names instead, use them as a guide to pipe over, or leave as impressions only.

CELEBROOKIES

This idea came to me in 2013, when I was asked by an accessories brand to make Katy Perry cookies for a product launch. In the end we used digital printed pictures, but I was later asked to make 'looky likey' cookies by a milk brand for a dunking cookie campaign. I had such fun making the famous faces, or 'celebrookies' as I liked to call them, from Stevie Wonder and Elvis to Miley Cyrus and Katy Perry. The project simply involves taking a clear photo, printing it out (you could make giant ones for a cake decoration), then drawing over some of the main features to give them a cartoony appearance. I chose my son George for this one, because he's got good hair that I thought would be fun to pipe. Make cookie caricatures of celebrities, or your own friends or family for a hilarious surprise treat. Pop them into bags as gifts if you are having a big decade celebration for a friend, or give out portraits to guests as a party favour. Don't be too worried about creating identical masterpieces! **Makes 20 cookies**

STUFF YOU'LL NEED

Equipment:
> your chosen picture, printed onto thin card, or paper that you have stuck to card (you'll need a few copies because we will cut the main shape, then cut into the card to make guides for marking out details)
> small scissors
> dark edible-ink pen

> piping bags and nozzles
> spare cake board
> small plate, to use as a paint palette
> fine paintbrushes

The Cookies:
> 1 quantity of Vanilla Cookie dough (see pages 213–14), rolled to guide-stick thickness, cut

around your chosen template and baked – mine were 11 cm (4½ in) top to bottom (see page 226 for template)

Ingredients:
> approx. 500 g (1 lb 2 oz) white royal icing (see page 188 for recipe and consistency guide, or use shop-bought)

> soft-peak royal icing and runny icing in colours of your choice (see step 04)
> dust colours for adding detail (I used Sugarflair in black, white, dusky pink and nutkin brown for the eyes, outlines, cheeks and lips)
> rejuvenator spirit

TIP › *If you prefer not to paint the pictures, send off your chosen image to 'edible' printers – there are loads of online services (see page 224). Alternatively, commission an artist to do a caricature or painting for you from a photo if you want to make a really special gift and aren't confident with painting. We sometimes work with a local artist, my friend Michelle, who specialises in portraits (see page 224). You can still cut out the person's shape from card on the cookie, then overlay the edible picture onto the shape, in the same way I used the edible print for the Doggy Biscuits on page 104.*

01. Lay your cooled cookie cut-outs on the work surface.

02. To create the face, cut out the whole face off the person in one of the card pictures (around the hairline

and chin, see pic 01 overleaf). Place the face on a cookie, lined up well, then draw around the top edge with an edible-ink pen to show the hairline, before tracing all around the face shape (see pic 02 overleaf). Do this on all of the cookies.

03. Using a piping bag fitted with a No. 2 nozzle, pipe the clothing outlines or neck detail. George's outfit was pretty simple to draw free-hand, but if your person is different, you may want to continue cutting out and tracing around a few of the larger key shapes, e.g. a neckline or a dress or sweater shape (do this in the same way you did the face), to be sure you've got everything in proportion. I added the white outline for his shirt and tie first (see pic 03 overleaf). →

04. Mix your icing colours: I used 2 tablespoons soft-peak white in a piping bag with a No. 2 nozzle; 2 tablespoons each of soft-peak royal icing in colours of your choice (I used grey and claret for the jacket and shirt) for outline detail; runny icing (let down soft-peak icing with a little water – see page 190) in colours of your choice for clothing; icing for skin tone (I used a tiny quantity of paprika/flesh paste colour and a little egg yellow); stiff-peak hair colour icing (I used chestnut and dark brown paste colour). For other hairstyles, try different nozzles – for smooth, long hair you could use soft-peak in a No. 3 nozzle, or for tight curls use stiff icing in a smaller nozzle (try out the hair on a work surface initially, piping from the scalp to the end points where you want the hair to finish).

~~~~~~~~

05. Once you've got the outlines piped on all your cookies, flood the face and neck (if you have any showing) in the skin-coloured royal icing (see pic 04). Leave to dry, ideally overnight, on a spare cake board.

NOTE

~~

If you are flooding two different colours, particularly strong contrasting ones, allow each coloured area to 'skin over' or dry for a few hours before piping the other colour next to it. This will prevent colour bleeding from one shape to another.

01

02

03

04

05

06

06. The next day, line up the photo next to a cookie. Take a very fine paintbrush and paint light grey shading for facial details (I used a gentle light wash of dust mixed with lots of rejuvenator spirit to create a light, watery paint). Mark out where the eyebrows, nose and mouth are, and details around the jawline and hairline (see pic 05).

07. Add a very light dusting of colour to the lips and cheek area (use a more striking colour if you are making a glam girl or similar) to mark out the shape, which you go over later with an outline to 'cartoonify' the face.

08. Pipe the hair, by piping strand upon strand and allowed each strand to end in a little point by stopping squeezing at the outer edge of the hair and pulling the piping bag off in the direction you wantthe hair to be (see pic 06). Flood the clothing in each colour, leaving time for each part to dry (see NOTE opposite).

09. Once the clothing is dry, use soft-peak icing in the same colour to outline each part of the garment. George has a boxy jacket on, so I piped lines for the lapel and tie to bring out the detail.

10. Make facial features – eyebrows, eyes, nose and mouth – 'pop' out by painting with dust colour, made into a thicker paint with rejuvenator spirit, using a very fine brush. Be careful not to overload the brush (see pic 07).

Ta-da! There you have it – a fun edible portrait.

WEDGWOOD-INSPIRED WHITE-ON-WHITE WEDDING CAKE

This cake is so elegant and classic. I got the inspiration from one of my past brides. She came to me with lots of pictures, including one of a hexagonal Martha Stewart cake (I just LOVE Martha Stewart, and in the States their cake work is phenomenal). I wanted to make the design my own, so I added Wedgwood-inspired detail in pure white. The white on ivory looks very ethereal, and although there is plenty of detail on the cake, because it is all pale it doesn't look fussy. The three panels of flower designs, used on alternate sides and tiers, are made using a crinkle circle cutter, a silicone rose mould and one of my favourite crafting techniques – quilling. I used to do quilling with my mum when I was little, and they transfer really well from paper to petal paste. The decoration is fairly straightforward but looks heavenly all together. Plan your time well – you can't rush this one!

STUFF YOU'LL NEED

Equipment:
› rolling pin
› large rose-shaped silicone mould (my mould is 5.5 cm/ 2 in across, and the rose shape within it is approx. 3 cm/1¼ in across)
› ribbon cutter
› small 6-petal metal cutter or similar ruffled flower cutter (mine were made with a 5 cm/2 in diameter flower cutter)
› rose-leaf plunger cutters (small and medium size)

› turntable
› side smoother
› pin tool or scriber needle
› small paintbrush
› cocktail sticks

The Cakes:
› 15 cm (6 in), 20 cm (8 in), 25 cm (10 in) and 30 cm (12 in) hexagonal cakes (any flavour you wish), split, filled and iced in ivory and stacked on a 40 cm (16 in) hexagonal cake board

Ingredients:
› icing (confectioners') sugar, for dusting
› decorations: moulded roses, ruffled florals and quilled panels (see pages 74–75)
› edible glue
› approx. 250 g (9 oz) white stiff-peak royal icing, in a piping bag with a No. 3 nozzle (see page 188 for recipe and consistency guide, or use shop-bought)

› 2 heaped tablespoons white soft-peak royal icing, in a piping bag with a No. 2 nozzle

NOTE

~~~

For decorating large cakes, I use one of those cheap TV turntables. They take a good weight and you can find them easily online (just search 'TV turntable').

Make these at least a couple of days ahead.

PUSH-MOULD ROSES

Dust the mould with icing sugar and tip out any excess. Take a little sugarpaste, about the size of a small hazelnut, and roll it into a ball. Push the sugarpaste into the mould with the base of your thumb, then use your fingertips to push it down into all the crevices. Turn the mould over. If you are lucky it will drop straight out onto the surface but if it doesn't, gently flex the mould one way then another. It should pop out easily if you've dusted the mould with icing sugar. Repeat until you have the number of roses you need, dusting the mould with icing sugar each time. I made eight large roses – two for each tier. Leave them to dry overnight.

TIP › *If your hands are hot or it's a hot day, the sugarpaste might be a bit sticky. If you do have trouble with it, use white modelling paste instead. It makes the job easier, but it is more expensive and also sets fairly hard over time.*

QUILLED PANELS

Dust the work surface with plenty of icing sugar and roll out 50 g (2 oz) petal or florist paste as thinly as possible. Using a ribbon cutter, cut several strips approx. 25 cm (10 in) long for the larger petals (you can cut them shorter for small leaves and stems), making sure you keep them all an equal width so they all stand out at the same distance from your cake. I used a ribbon cutter on a thin setting then split these in half by eye, but you can use a really thin setting for each strip if you find it hard to judge this. To create the shapes, turn the strip on its side and roll it into a tight coil. Unravel as required to loosen, pinching off at one end to create teardrop shape patterns, allowing small gaps within the strip to show. Use a little edible glue, if necessary, to secure each cut end. If you have excess strips, turn them into smaller leaves, heart shapes or stems. Make various shapes and sizes – you can be very free-form with these. For the structured designs on the panels you need one large 5-petal quilled bloom with smaller leaves and shaped stems coming from this central design (I made about 40 petals, 10 stems, and 30 leaves or small filler shapes). Leave to dry for at least two days on a spare cake board dusted with icing sugar.

RUFFLE FLORALS

To create each large floral bloom, dust the work surface with plenty of icing sugar and roll out 50 g (2 oz) petal paste as thinly as possible. Cut three small six-petal flowers with your cutter. Fold each one in half. Pipe a tiny pearl of royal icing at the bottom of each one on one side while they lay on the work surface in front of you. Gather the halves and pinch together at the bottom where the icing is, to secure them. Now open them out slightly. Leave to set overnight or for a couple of days. For smaller buds, simply crinkle up a single flower shape from the centre, to make a small ruffled loose bloom, allowing the petals to go in any direction. Pinch in a little at the centre with your fingertips to mould it and hold it in shape. Leave to dry with the larger ones.

To make leaves, use the same thin rolled-out petal paste and cut out a few medium and small leaves with the rose-leaf plunger cutters (or similar leaf cutter) – about 20 of each size will do (six for each panel). Leave the leaves to set along with the flowers. Give each one a delicate twist or lift at their ends to add a some movement. →

ASSEMBLE THE CAKE

TIP › *Before you begin, check you don't have any large gaps between the tiers where you'll be piping the pearl trim. If you do, use some royal icing to fill the gaps.*

01. Place the cake tiers on a turntable. Score a guideline on your cake with the side smoother and a pin tool, to mark out straight lines on the cake tiers just within each corner angle, on every other cake side, so you have a panel then a space, and repeat (see pic 01). Each tier will have three piped 'snail trail' panels. You want to have the panel below being a blank one if the panel directly above has got the panel piped. Score the lines on all of the tiers.

02. Pipe the 'snail trail' over the scored boxes on the panels with the stiff-peak royal icing (see pic 02 and page 193 for technique). (Don't pipe around the tier edges just yet as you'll do that when you attach the floral designs.)

Come in close into your cake, and at a 45-degree angle, pipe a stiff pearl from your piping bag on the cake at one top corner, drawing the nozzle away from the pearl to create a 'tail'. Piping a line of pearls from the top of the tier to the bottom, release the pressure slightly as you drag the nozzle downwards, piping pearls that slightly overlap the bottom of the tail of the previous pearl. Continue until you have a beaded 'snail trail' following the scored line from the top of the cake tier to the bottom where it meets the tier below. Carry on the boxed

shape, bringing your nozzle back to the top edge where you started the first trail, piping a pearl along the top edge at the same angle. Repeat all the way along the line you have scored on this first cake side until you reach the next corner. Stop with a tail at the end. Now finish the boxed effect by piping a third line downwards on your next corner to the bottom of the tier. Leave the side of the cake next to this panel blank, turn the cake around and repeat over your scored lines to create the next panel. Repeat this all over the tiers in the same way, leaving a blank panel between each piped one.

03. Add your decorations, sticking on the moulded roses first, using a dab of stiff royal icing on the back of each one (see pic 03). I used the front to display one rose on my top tier within a piped panel, then another rose within the piped panel at the front of my cake on the third tier down. Then I added two further roses on the panels below the top tier on either side, and repeated this pattern by adding two more on the base tier either side of the central panel (see picture opposite).

04. Attach the separate quilled petals and stems in an arrangement you like on each of the panels on each tier (alternate the designs so you have one large quilled arrangement on the centre at the front of the second tier down), using a little edible glue or thin royal icing with a

01

02

03

paintbrush, along with the rose and floral designs. I used two per tier for each style of decoration. Arrange the quills in a large group of five and add the smaller leaves and stems to fill where you like. If you find you get the odd larger quill or petal slipping, use a cocktail stick to hold it in place just underneath the shape overnight, and remove the stick the next day once the glue or icing is set.

~~~~~~~~

05. Finally, add the ruffle floral panels. Using royal icing, attach the large and small blooms where you wish. Using soft-peak royal icing in piping bag fitted with a No. 2 nozzle, pipe stems from the blooms in a swirly line down to the tier below so it looks like they are growing up the tier from the base. Add some filler stems. To pipe these, bring the nozzle in close to the cake, just under the base of the flower, and pipe a line/stem down in a swirling motion to the point where the stem finished. Repeat as necessary to make the pattern flow from the flowers over the panel. Make swirly tendrils and add your leaves to the design where you like. You can also add pretty 'triple dot' royal icing pearls. I love to use these to fill gaps on my cakes.

~~~~~~~~

06. To finish, pipe a 'pearl snail' in white over the panel-edges and joints of each tier. Less pressure will create tiny pearls; more pressure will create larger pearls. Once you are happy with the size, stop squeezing and swiftly pull the piping bag away from the pearl. You may get a little peak or 'tail' (we call these 'nipples' in the trade). If you do, just dampen a paintbrush and press them in to round off the pearl and push in the little peak.

TOP TIP

~~~

Always work from the top of the cake down, so that when you are piping on the tier above, you don't smudge any piping with your hands on the tier below.

Dot the moulded roses on alternating panels for a pleasing pattern.

NOT-SO-DIRTY BURGER

What's not to like about this cake? We've seen a huge trend for meat and burgers over the past few years, and this cake could be made for so many occasions. We made a lovely burger cake for a four-year-old's birthday who dreamed of having his own burger bar: my mate Dan P Carter, an amazing artist, sculpted a true-to-life burger and bun, and we used Belgian Chocolate Brownie Torte Cake for the patties (see page 209) and Vanilla Bean Sponge (see page 200) for the bun. I love this sculpted cake because the shapes are so simple, and, as a burger is naturally a bit lumpy and bumpy, you don't need to worry about getting everything neat and perfect. It's a great cake to make if you are new to airbrushing or sculpting. If you don't have an airbrush machine, simply add detail using dust colours on a dry pastry brush and keep building up the colour by hand. I went for a classic gingham American diner-style 'burger' with edible paper in red check for the base. The marzipan chips really make this design. They are so easy to make and look very realistic.

STUFF YOU'LL NEED

Equipment:

› 18 cm (7 in) and 15 cm (6 in) thin round cake cards
› bread knife or serrated palette knife
› modelling tool with pointed tip (such as a Dresden tool)
› cake smoothers
› rolling pin
› guide sticks
› large cake board, for the chips
› turntable
› airbrush machine (see page 224 for stockists)
› 40 cm (16 in) round cake drum, iced in white sugarpaste (see pages 182–85), plus spare cake drum in the same size
› 23 cm (9 in) cake drum, for cutting cheese squares out with
› small, sharp knife
› 7 cm (3 in) round cutter

for the tomatoes (or you can cut them by hand)
› cake dowel
› hacksaw
› 6 cm (2½ in) round cutter, for the gherkins (optional)

The Cakes:

› 20 cm- (8 in-) tall, deep round cake made with 1.5 kg (3 lb 5 oz) Vanilla Bean Sponge mix (see page 200), which will be split in half leaving the top layer with the round hump un-trimmed to create the rounded bun top shape
› 18 cm (7 in) round cake made with 650 g (1 lb 7 oz) Belgian Chocolate Brownie Torte Cake batter, for the 'patty', leveled and split in half

Ingredients:

› 100 g (3½ oz) chocolate buttercream (see page 218) for filling the 'patty' cake, and 250 g (9 oz) vanilla buttercream (see page 216) for filling the 'bun' halves
› a little just-boiled apricot jam
› icing (confectioners') sugar, for dusting
› 2.5 kg (5 lb 8 oz) marzipan
› vodka or cooled boiled water
› 2 kg (4 lb 6 oz) white sugarpaste
› airbrush colours (I used water-based Kroma colours in yellow, red and brown)
› edible printed gingham check (optional) (see page 81 for template)
› 2 teaspoons stiff white royal icing (see page 188 for recipe and consistency guide, or use

shop-bought)
› extra sugarpaste for 'burger' accessories – I used egg yellow for the 'cheese', Christmas red for the 'tomatoes', a marbled mix of white, yellow and mint gooseberry paste colour for the 'lettuce' and mint paste for the gherkins
› 2 tablespoons soft royal icing, coloured with Christmas red and egg yellow for pale 'burger mayo'
› 3 tablespoons bright red soft-peak royal icing (Christmas red paste colour) for the 'ketchup'
› 1 heaped tablespoon soft-peak royal icing coloured with a little egg-yellow and caramel-ivory paste colour, to create pale sesame seeds, in a piping bag fitted with a No. 2 nozzle

01. Start by splitting both vanilla sponges in half again so you can fill each part of the 'bun' with some buttercream. Fill the sponges with buttercream (the top and bottom of the 'bun' in your vanilla sponge layers and the chocolate cake for your 'patty') then stick the 'bun' cakes to their thin cake cards with a little buttercream and chill all the cakes for an hour. The card helps keep the cake stable when moving it from the decorating board onto the main cake board, and adds →

01

02

03

04

05

06

support to the cake when it is stacked together. Sculpt the 'bun' and 'patty' shapes from the chilled sponges (the top of the 'bun' is the domed cake), carving with a bread knife or serrated palette knife to make basic rounded shapes. Place the sculpted cakes back in the fridge to chill.

~~~~~~~~

02. Brush each sponge with the hot jam, knead the marzipan, then dust the work surface with icing sugar and roll out the marzipan for each sponge to guide-stick thickness. Use

cake smoothers to help shape the cakes. Cover the 'burger', tucking the marzipan under. While the 'buns' set, use the modelling tool to sculpt lines and detail onto the outside edges of the 'patty', to create a textured 'meaty' pattern (see pic 01). Leave overnight.

~~~~~~~~

03. Ice both 'buns' with sugarpaste, using smoothers to create the shape. Leave them to set again overnight. Roll out the remaining marzipan in thick slabs and cut into uneven 'chip' shapes with a small, sharp knife (see pic 02).

Place on the large cake board, which you've dusted with a little icing sugar.

~~~~~~~~

04. The next day, finish your creation, ideally using a turntable so you can spin the cakes around while lightly spraying them with colour. Start with the 'buns' and 'chips'. Keep the airbrush gun about 30 cm (12 in) away from the sponges so you get an even and light colour that you can gradually build upon. (If you haven't used an airbrush before, practice on blank paper or an old cake-box lid.) Half-fill the well of the gun with liquid colour

07

(I used yellow first) and spray over the tops of the 'buns', leaving the bottoms a little whiter (see pic 03). You will probably need to re-fill the well a few times. Once you have a light yellow tone over the top and sides, use brown liquid colour to add the baked crusty look to the top of the bun: keep the gun a good distance away and gradually build up the 'baked' look. Leave to dry for about 30 minutes. Lay out the 'chips' and lightly spray them with yellow, then brown, to give them a little golden tinge, turning them to colour all sides. The airbrush colours naturally fall more on the sharp edges of the chips, making them look even more real. Leave them to dry for about 30 minutes.

TIP › *Pop the sprayed pieces onto a sheet of baking parchment to protect the surface – the colours are quite strong.*

05. Now, colour the burger. I used yellow and brown first, to build up a little colour, then sprayed red over the blotchy patches, coming in closer to the burger. Continue spraying with brown and red until you have a nice 'juicy' chargrilled burger effect (see pic 04). Come in closer to the burger to get some shading. Leave to dry for at least 1 hour. →

GINGHAM TEMPLATE

08

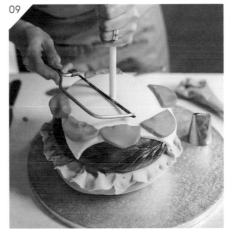

09

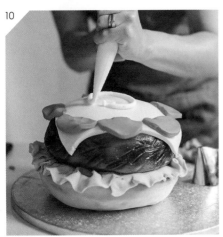

10

11

06. Pop the bottom of the 'bun' onto a cake board. Adorn your burger with all the trimmings: roll out the marbled sugarpaste for the lettuce thinly, in strips a few inches wide. Lay all around the edge of the base 'bun', using folds to create a ruffled effect. Pop the 'burger' on top (see pics 05 and 06 on previous page).

~~~~~~~

07. Now for the cheesy action: roll out the yellow sugarpaste larger than the 'burger' (I used a spare square 23 cm (9 in) cake drum to cut around). Cut out the 'cheese' and lay it over the 'burger' (see pic 07).

~~~~~~~

08. Roll out a small handful of red sugarpaste in a thick layer, cut out 7 cm (3 in) circles, then

halve these to create semi-circle 'tomato' slices to arrange around the edge of the burger (see pic 08). For an extra authenticity, add 'gherkin' slices to your burger, alternating them with the tomato slices. Make them in the same way you made the tomatoes but use a green coloured sugarpaste and the 6 cm (2½ in) pastry cutter.

~~~~~~~

09. Plunge the cake dowel down the middle of the 'burger and bun' and use the hacksaw to mark the point where the dowel exits the top layer (see pic 09). Take it out, cut it down to this height, then pop it back into the sponge. Pipe a little royal icing on the 'cheese' before sitting the top 'bun on top' (see pics 10 and 11). The card under the top bun helps support the structure.

12

10. Transfer the cake to an iced board (see NOTE). Pipe 'burger mayo' onto the 'lettuce' under the burger, and finish with some piped 'ketchup' on the top area, to create the effect that these sauces are oozing out of your 'patty and bun' (see pic 12). Add 'sesame seeds' with stiff royal icing in a piping bag with a No. 2 nozzle (pipe pearls, releasing pressure and drawing back, to create tear-drop shapes, see pic 13). Lay the chips around the burger (see pic 14). If you like, you can add a piped message using the 'ketchup' to personalise the design. Who can resist taking a bite out of this!

13

14

NOTE

~~~

To ice a cake drum see steps on pages 184–85. For a real 'all-American' diner look, use edible gingham check paper (see page 81 for the template). Carefully set your 'burger' on the iced board sitting slightly to the back to allow room for the 'chips'.

PAINTED & PRINTED BIRDS

I specialise in hand-painted cakes, and love making them – they look so elegant. This cake was inspired by one of my early painted bird designs, and offers a 'cheat' way to create a painted cake, using a mix of edible print and hand-painting. You can find gorgeous pictures online, or why not take your own pictures of birds? Because all of the detail is printed for you (you can order printed sheets online – see page 224 for stockists), this looks really stunning, and the hand-painted branches give it a really clever finish. Most people assume it's all hand painted! You can embellish the printed pictures by painting on the pictures themselves, picking out certain colours or details. This is a lovely quick and easy way to decorate cakes.

STUFF YOU'LL NEED

Equipment:
› good-quality fine paintbrushes, in various sizes
› a plate to use as a paint pallet
› scissors
› length of 1 cm (½ in) brown ribbon

The Cakes
› 10 cm (4 in), 15cm (6 in) and 20 cm (8 in) round cakes, iced in a powder blue/grey

(I used Renshaw duck-egg blue with a little black kneaded into it to create a light blue shade), stacked on a 28 cm (11 in) iced and ribboned drum (see pages 182–85)

Ingredients:
› edible paint dust colours for the branches and leaves (I used Sugarflair blossom dusts in nutkin brown, dusky pink, black, white, spruce and apple green)

› rejuvenator spirit
› printed edible pictures of birds
› vodka or cooled boiled water
› a little stiff royal icing, for sticking (see page 188 for recipe and consistency guide, or use shop-bought)

---

01. Mix your paint dust colours (see pic 01 overleaf). Choose the front of your cake where it looks best. Paint branches on the cake, using a fairly watered-down mix of paint dust and rejuvenator spirit (see pic 02 overleaf). It looks good to have branches stemming from the bottom in thicker parts, starting like a thicker tree stump, then thinning out as the branches climb over and up towards the top edge of the tiers, making the branches more delicate as you get higher up. You can do this initially with a fairly light wash to plan out where you want to paint the branches. Make sure that where you paint your branches, there is the right amount of space left so that your printed bird pictures will not bend over the top edge of the tier.

02. Outline the branches in thicker, darker brown paint and add depth and shading (see pic 03 overleaf). I used pink, brown and white to create lighter bits of the branches near the tops, and I cross-hatch shading on the lower parts of the branches to show shadow. Paint leaves by hand in pale green and add detail to the centres and edges once you've placed the basic shapes on the cake. Add more detail if you wish – perhaps blossoms or tendrils coming from the main branches. →

03. Once you've painted branches over the cake, cut out your birds (if the feet are fragile, leave them and paint them on later), then carefully dampen the back of them with a little water around the edge of the shape (see pic 04). Gently press each one in place on the cake. If they aren't quite sticking, paint the backs with thinned-out royal icing but be careful not to make them too damp as the pictures can dissolve easily. If you need to, paint the birds' feet, wrapping them over the branches to appear like they are grasping on. I used hand painting to enhance the eyes, feet and beaks on my birds (see pics 05 and 06). Finish the cake by adding ribbon around each tier (adhere it with a dab of royal icing on the back of the cake).

'WORLD'S BEST DAD' CHOCOLATE MINI BITES

'Hey, it's George here, Juliet's son. My mum's been running a bakery for years now and people always assume I get loads of cake! If I wanted to I could probably go in every day and stuff my face with cupcakes, but we've grown up with baking so I guess we're just used to getting awesome cakes for our birthdays. Anyway, I decided to knock up some mini-chocolate cakes for Dad last Father's Day. I must admit, having an expert baker for a mum did help, but after I'd made them and realised how easy it was, I knew anyone could make them! So when Mum asked if I'd contribute a recipe to the book, I thought this would be perfect. So here they are: mini chocolate ganache cakes. I added a bit of Dad's favourite whisky to the ganache and the buttercream, to make them special for him.' **Makes 16–20 mini bites**

STUFF YOU'LL NEED

Equipment:
› 5 cm (2 in) round cutter
› pastry brush
› rolling pin
› small, sharp knife
› 2 side smoothers
› baking parchment
› wire cooling rack
› presentation board or large platter or ice a rectangle cake drum (see pages 182–85)

or use paper, like our world map design here, to pick out one of your dad's favourite things

The Cake:
› Belgian Chocolate Brownie Torte Cake (see page 209) baked in a 25 cm/10 in square tin, split in half

Ingredients:
› a little just-boiled apricot jam
› icing (confectioners') sugar, for dusting
› approx. 500 g (1 lb 2 oz) marzipan
› Chocolate Pouring Ganache (see page 222), flavoured with Dad's favourite whisky, to taste
› selection of coloured soft-peak royal icing in piping bags with a No. 2 nozzle

(1 heaped tablespoon of each is plenty – I used ice blue, tangerine and bitter lemon – see page 188 for recipe or use shop-bought)

---

01. Fill the cake with the buttercream of your choice and chill for an hour (I used a whisky-flavoured chocolate buttercream).

02. Once chilled, use the round cutter to cut out 16–20 bite-sized circles of cake (see pic 01 overleaf).

TIP › *If you find the chocolate cake sticky, dip your cutter in hot boiled water between each cut.*

03. Brush each cake with the apricot jam to make them sticky (see pic 02 overleaf).

04. Knead the marzipan, then dust the work surface with icing sugar and roll it out to a thin layer of about 2–3 mm (see pic 03 overleaf). Cut out rough shapes large enough to cover the top and sides of your cakes; 15 cm (6 in) squares are good. Lay a piece of marzipan over the top of a cake circle, and smooth down the sides with your fingers. Use side smoothers to neatly press the marzipan against the cake edges fairly firmly, removing any creases (see pic 04 overleaf). Cut around the bottom of the cake's edge with a sharp knife, smooth again and pat down the top to flatten. Transfer to a piece of baking parchment. Repeat with the remaining squares of marzipan and circles of cake. Leave all of your cakes to set for a few hours or overnight. →

01

02

03

04

~~~~~~~~~

05. Next, cover the cakes with the ganache. Lay a sheet of baking parchment on the work surface and cover with a wire cooling rack. Line up the cakes on the rack. Once you've made the pouring ganache, let it to cool a little, transfer it to a jug, then generously pour it over the cakes (see pic 05). Make sure you pour it over all sides to completely coat each little cake. Once they're all covered, gently tap the wire rack against the work surface (see pic 06). This will encourage the ganache to pour over and sit smoothly, with any excess running off the sides. Stop once all the cakes look lovely and glossy. (The excess ganache that drips onto the paper can be re-bagged and kept in the fridge for up to 1 week or frozen for 1 month.) Leave the cakes to set on the rack for 1–2 hours, depending on the temperature in the room. Ideally don't chill them or you may cause the chocolate coating to bloom.

06. Once set, use a small, sharp knife or palette knife to lift each cake from the rack and pop onto your serving platter or board. Pipe any message you like over your cakes (see pic 07). These are perfect for Father's Day so we've spelt out 'World's Best Dad' by piping a large letter on the top of each cake, but you could equally make these for a birthday or Mother's Day, perhaps even adding chocolate flowers to the top of each one. Once covered, the cakes will last for a few days. You might find the coating blooms over time but it will still taste delicious.

06

07

PIÑATA SURPRISE

Piñata cakes are very 'in' right now but I think these fabulous cakes with a surprise are bound to stay around for years to come. They are such fun, and really add a surprise element to any party. I want to try a multi-tiered version filled with wedding favours; I will get round to it eventually! This cake looks impressive, but is actually very simple to make. The most time-consuming task is dyeing all of the buttercream and loading it into piping bags, but once you've done the prep, the piping of the ruffles is very quick. You could make this project in any colours. I've gone for a traditional Mexican vibe, but you could use all pinks, or the colours of a company logo, or all white for a wedding. It really doesn't matter if it's not perfect or super neat, as all the colours and ruffles look great together: any imperfections or unlevelled lines merge into the one design.

STUFF YOU'LL NEED

Equipment:
› large cake leveller or bread knife
› 30 cm (12 in) round cake card
› turntable (optional)
› approx. 15 cm (6 in) diameter plate or cake board
› palette knife
› large plastic piping bags

› (1 for each colour of buttercream)
› large petal nozzles to create ruffles (1 for each colour of buttercream)

The Cakes:
› 2 x deep 30 cm (12 in) round Vanilla Bean Sponge cakes (see page 200) – 2.2 kg (4 lb 14 oz) cake mix in each tin gives a good depth, as you need to split them in half to create the cavity for the sweets

Ingredients:
› 2.5 kg (5 lb 8 oz) buttercream in various bright colours: equal amounts in orange, blue, purple, yellow and red (I used Sugarflair tangerine, grape violet, ice blue, Christmas red and egg yellow)
› plenty of sweets of your choice

01. Cut the rounded top off each cake using a cake leveller or bread knife, leaving the sponges as deep as possible (see pic 01 overleaf). Cut each sponge in half through the middle again, so you now have 4 discs of sponge (see pic 02 overleaf).

02. Take both of the centre layers of sponge and stack them on the work surface so the top sponge is completely covering the bottom sponge. Pop the plate or board onto the top, right in the centre. Now, using a bread knife, cut right through both layers, around the plate or board, to create the circular ring pieces for your sweet cavity (see pic 03 overleaf).

03. Place one of the un-cut sponge layers, crust-side down, on the 30 cm (12 in) cake card. Use a little buttercream to stick it in place. Place the board and cake on a turntable. This will be your bottom layer.

04. Place the plate or board on the bottom layer sitting on the cake card, and mark out the area that you need to see for your buttercream filling (see pic 04 overleaf). Spread buttercream around the edge, just outside that circle area you've marked out, with a palette knife. (I used a jolly orange buttercream for mine, see pic 05 overleaf.)

05. Pop the second layer onto the base. Carefully lift it with the inner circle cut but not removed, so the →

layer doesn't break. Remove the cut circle (see pics 06 and 07). Spread buttercream around the edge of the sponge (see pic 08). Repeat with the third layer. Freeze the cut circles or use to make different cake another time. Now it's ready to pack full of goodies!

~~~~~~~~~~

06. Fill the cavity with sweets (see pic 09). Close the piñata by adding the final layer (see pic 10 overleaf). Spread a fine coating of buttercream all over the cake with a palette knife to crumb coat (see pic 11 overleaf). →

01

02

03

04

05

06

07

08

09

10

11

07. For the decorative ruffle rings around the cake, begin at the bottom of the cake and hold the piping bag fitted with the petal nozzle against the sponge. Make sure that the wider fat point is touching the cake and the thin part of the nozzle is facing outwards. Use a wiggly, wavy motion as you pipe around the cake edge to create a ruffly effect, making sure the narrow part of the nozzle is still facing out. Once you've finished the first layer and returned to your starting point, change colours (if using more than one colour) and pipe the next wiggly ruffle line above the first, so it looks like a real piñata! Continue with as many colours as you like until you've covered the side of the cake (see pics 12 and 13). Once you reach the top, continue piping ruffles around the edge, but now come into the centre of the cake by piping smaller and smaller circles until you get to the middle. Olé! A perfect piñata cake ready for a show-stopping surprise at any event!

12

13

SEA SALTED CARAMEL SEASIDE CUPCAKES

Living by the seaside, we all love a bit of seaside kitsch. These fun, simple cupcakes are perfect to take down to our beach hut, or for kid's parties, and they taste amazing. Using silicone moulds to create sugarpaste shells and creatures is really easy, but if you don't have silicone moulds, shell shapes are easy to make by moulding the paste with your fingers into basic cones and shells before adding detail with modelling tools. They have a delicious salted caramel topping sprinkled with chunky flakes of pure sea salt. **Makes approximately 12–16 cupcakes**

STUFF YOU'LL NEED

Equipment:
> selection of shell and sea-creature silicone moulds (see page 224 for stockists)
> paintbrushes
> plate to use as a paint palette
> large piping bag with an open star nozzle

The Cupcakes:
> 12–16 caramel Vanilla Bean Sponge cupcakes (see variation on page 204)

Ingredients:
> icing (confectioners') sugar, for dusting
> 80 g (3 oz) each of white or ivory, pale blue and pale lilac sugarpaste
> selection of dust colours for adding detail (I've used orange, red, yellows, blues, black, purple and green for clown fish, shells, seahorses and octopuses but use any colours you like)
> rejuvenator spirit

> approx. 600 g (1 lb 5 oz) salted caramel buttercream (see page 218)
> 2 tablespoons caramel (good-quality shop-bought caramel sauce or see page 219 for recipe)
> golden caster (superfine) sugar, for the sand effect
> sea salt flakes

01. Start by making your seaside decorations. (You can make them a few weeks in advance, as they keep for ages in a cake box.) Dust the clean moulds with a little icing sugar and pat out the excess. Knead the sugarpaste (I've used ivory for shells, blue for seahorses and lilac for the octopus) on a work surface dusted with icing sugar then break off a small piece. Push the sugarpaste firmly into the mould until it's filled to the top, making sure all the crevices are filled. Then lift the mould, turn it over and tap the sugarcraft shape out onto the surface (see pic 01 overleaf). If they stick, gently flex the moulds to encourage them to pop out. (See page 74 for step-by-step visuals on using a silicone mould.) Repeat, until you have prepared all your seaside decorations. Leave them to dry for at least 24 hours before decorating with dusts.

02. Add detail to the sugarcraft seaside decorations with dust colours (see pic 02 overleaf). The indentations and moulded parts will grab a bit more colour as you dust with

your paintbrush, or you can create edible paints (for the clown fish I used rejuvenator spirit and bright orange dust to give them orange stripes, and made black paint for the lines and eye details). Have fun with these; they are simple to make, and once they are all together they look fab. The shells are easy: just dust over the curved shells and the edges.

03. Top the cupcakes with buttercream: Pipe the buttercream from above, around the edge of the cupcake case, then continue to wind around to the centre to make a soft whipped topping. Drizzle with a little caramel sauce (ideally from a piping bag, see pic 03 overleaf), then sprinkle generously with golden caster sugar (edible sand), and top with flakes of sea salt (see pic 04).

04. Adorn your delicious sweet and salty morsels with the sugarcraft shells and creatures to finish. Enjoy!

01

02

03

TOP TIP

~~~

It's easier to give
them a thin drizzle
from a piping bag
than from a
spoon.

04

DOGGY BISCUITS

These snazzy cookies look great, and are so simple to make. I've made many variations but I love Dalmatians. My daughter Lydia designed the spotty print for me on the computer (see template on the next page), but you could use any print pattern you like. The edible printed sheets are finished with a tiny bit of piping detail to bring out the face and add collars. These make great gifts for so many occasions, especially for dog lovers! **Makes 4 biscuits**

STUFF YOU'LL NEED

Equipment:
› rolling pin
› pastry brush
› palette knife
› shop-bought dog-shaped cutter, or use a card template on page 226

› scalpel or small, sharp knife (optional)
› cake smoother

The Biscuits:
› 4 Dalmatian-shaped baked biscuits (I used Vanilla Cookies, see page 213)

Ingredients:
› icing (confectioners') sugar, for dusting
› 250 g (9 oz) white sugarpaste
› vodka or cooled boiled water
› a little white soft-peak royal icing, in a piping bag (see page 188 for recipe and consistency guide, or use shop-bought),

for sticking
› A4 sheet of edible Dalmatian print (see page 107)
› 2 tablespoons soft-peak royal icing, one coloured with black and the other with mint paste colour in piping bags fitted with No. 2 nozzles for the face and collar detail

01. Liberally dust the work surface with icing sugar and roll out the sugarpaste very thinly, until it's just over A4 size, and as thin as a sheet of dried lasagne (until you can just see the work surface showing through the sugarpaste – see pic 01 overleaf).

02. Brush a little vodka or cooled boiled water over the surface of the icing to make it tacky (see pic 02 overleaf). The edible sheets are fairly sticky, so don't make the icing too wet.

03. Using a palette knife, carefully push it under the outer edge of the edible paper and lift the paper from its plastic backing (see pic 03 overleaf). Take care not to tear it as it is fairly delicate. Lift the whole sheet away from the backing and lay it over the damp sugarpaste in one direction, using your fingertips to push out any air bubbles.

04. Using the cutter, press out the dog shapes, cutting right through the edible print and the sugarpaste (see pic 04 overleaf). If you decide to use a card template, use a scalpel or small, very sharp knife to cut around the shape as many times as you need.

05. Pipe a little white royal icing around the outer edge and middle of each biscuit (see pic 05 overleaf). If you are making tons of these, then make just 10 at a time as the icing will dry after a few minutes.

06. Place each printed piece of sugarpaste onto the biscuits, lining them up neatly and pressing them on firmly with a smoother (see pic 06 overleaf).

07. Pipe a nose, eye and ear shape with black icing and, finally, finish off with a jolly green collar and buckle (see pic 07 overleaf). Leave to dry overnight and display or wrap as required. →

NOTE
~~~
An A4 sheet of edible print
is enough to make 4 dogs.
Print more sheets if required.
It's always worth having a
few spare, just in case you
make a mistake!

01

02

03

04

**TOP TIP**

~~~

Using edible printed sheets
is fairly straightforward, but if the
printed sheet is a little sticky when
you remove it from its backing,
pop it in a very low oven at
50–60°C (120–140°F) for
2–3 minutes to dry out
a touch.

05

06

07

SPOT TEMPLATE

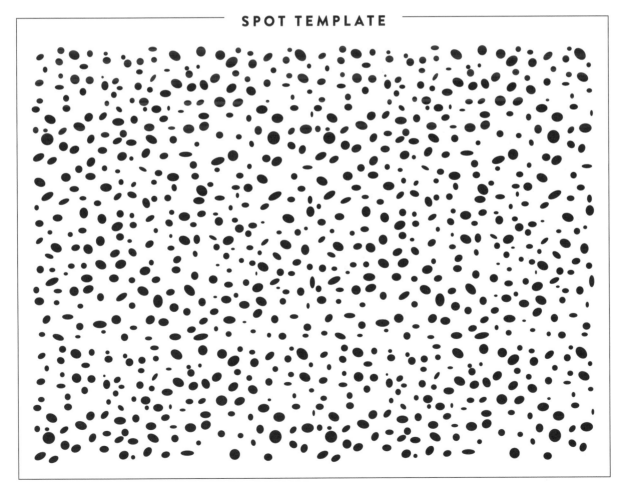

ACID BRIGHTS BUTTERCREAM CAKE

This is one of my favourite ways to decorate a buttercream cake. I love bright acid neon colours, so I've really gone for it with the colour scheme. This looks lovely in many variations, from bright red through all the pink shades, or even grey to white. Once you've prepared the buttercream shades, the decorating is very quick, and it's a rough design, so you don't have to be too fussy about the finish. It's an ideal cake to decorate and transport in separate tiers: once at your venue you can simply stack them and add buttercream pearl trims over the joins. The cake needs a lot of sponge, so you can always make these in advance and freeze them until you're ready to construct the cake.

STUFF YOU'LL NEED

Equipment:
› 7 large plastic piping bags
› 15 cm (6 in), 20 cm (8 in) and 25 cm (10 in) round pieces of cake card
› baking parchment
› 3 spare cake boards, larger than each tier you are decorating
› turntable
› medium and large palette knife
› side scraper
› small, sharp knife

› spare bowl
› cake dowels
› cake stand or iced cake board, wider than the bottom tier
› 3 x small piping bags with No. 3 nozzles for piping the buttercream pearl trims

The Cakes:
› 15 cm (6 in), 20 cm (8 in) and 25 cm (10 in) round vanilla sponges, each baked in 2 tins, then split, filled and crumb-

coated (see pages 168–71 for technique), chilled

Ingredients:
› approx. 3.7 kg (8 lb 3 oz) Vanilla Bean Buttercream (see page 216)
› assorted paste colours – you'll need 7 colours for this 3-tier cake (I used tangerine/apricot paste colour for the top orange shade and bitter lemon/lime for the strongest shade – just 2 colours – and mixed them

with plain buttercream to make the other shades)
› a little stiff royal icing (see page 188 for recipe and consistency guide, or use shop-bought)

01. Start by preparing all of your buttercream shades. Make up each colour then spoon each shade into a large plastic piping bag without a nozzle (snip the ends off to pipe). You need a lot more buttercream for the bottom tier shades than you do for the top tier. It's best to make more than you need, as you need plenty of buttercream in each bag in order to pipe with an even pressure and the same thickness around the cake. You use the colour from the top of the bottom tier, to go around the base of the tier above, so you don't

want to run out of a shade. You can re-use all of the leftover buttercream: freeze it or use it for cupcakes!

Use the picture on the next page as a guide for the colour shades and colour the buttercream by eye, stirring in paste colour little by little until you have achieved a good shade. →

~~~~~~~~~

BRIGHT TANGERINE

01. Approx. 400 g (14 oz) of bright tangerine buttercream, for the top and upper layer of colour on the top tier.

PALE ORANGE

02. Approx. 200 g (7 oz) of bright tangerine buttercream mixed into white to make a lighter orange for the middle ring of colour on the top tier.

PEACH

03. Approx. 700 g (1 lb 9 oz) of a lighter peachy shade using a small quantity of leftover shade 2 above, mixed into plain white buttercream, for the bottom of the top tier, and to cover the top of tier two and the upper layer. Reserve the remaining buttercream to pipe the trim around the bottom of the top tier.

CREAMY/NATURAL

04. Approx. 350 g (12 oz) of plain vanilla buttercream, no colour added, for the middle ring of colour on the middle tier.

PASTEL LEMON

05. Approx. 1 kg (2 lb 3 oz) of a pale bitter lemon shade (I used a small amount of bitter lemon/lime paste colour) for the bottom of the middle tier, and to cover the top and upper layer of the bottom tier. Reserve the remaining buttercream to pipe the trim around the bottom of the middle tier.

PALE LEMON/LIME

06. Approx. 500 g (1 lb 2oz) of a light green shade for the middle of the bottom tier (use more bitter lemon/lime paste colour to dye the buttercream darker).

BITTER LEMON/LIME

07. Approx. 500 g (1 lb 2oz) of a really bright lime shade for the bottom of the base tier. Reserve the remaining buttercream to pipe the trim around the base of the bottom tier.

02. Now you have done the laborious bit, you can get cracking with the buttercream covering. Place one of your cakes on a spare card lined with baking parchment-covered board and cake turntable (I've started with the top tier). Start with your bottom ring of colour, so for me this was the peach shade, and snip off the end of the piping bag so you have a hole about 1 cm (½ in) across. Pipe it all the way around the base of the cake, spinning the turntable as you go to give a thick sausage-like coating around the bottom. Continue building up these rough piped rings of buttercream to about a third of the way up the cake. Set the piping bag to one side; you will need some of it for the pearl trim.

03. Continue with the second shade up, piping a few rings all around the cake, so you have the cake covered about two thirds of its depth (see pic 01).

04. To finish the cake tier, take the final shade and continue with the piped rings around the top of the tier and continue to pipe in decreasing circles over the top, making sure to keep a nice even pressure so you have an even thickness layer on the top (see pics 02 and 03).

05. With your palette knife, use a firm pressure to neatly paddle out the buttercream on the top, using a pushing action at a fairly close angle to your cake, to flatten the top covering. Get it as smooth as you can (see pic 04).

06. Now, hold your side scraper up to the cake and, keeping it as straight and vertical as possible (holding it at about a 45-degree angle and facing away from you), →

BITTER
LEMON/
LIME

PASTEL
LEMON

PALE
LEMON/LIME

CREAMY/
NATURAL

TOP TIP

~~~

Make more buttercream than you need in order to pipe with an even pressure and the same thickness around the cake.

PALE ORANGE

PEACH

BRIGHT TANGERINE

sweep it continuously all around the cake until you reach your starting point (see pic 05 on previous page). Once you meet the starting point, quickly pull the scraper away from the cake. You'll be left with a straight line mark where the scraper has left the buttercream. Scrape off the excess buttercream from your scraper into the spare bowl. Be sure to wash and dry the scraper before using it on the other tiers.

Now you should have a neat cake with a smooth side with a blended three-shade coating. Remove any odd bits of buttercream poking up over the top by holding a small, sharp knife at a flat angle in line with the top edge of the cake and carefully trimming off any excess buttercream (see pic 06 on previous page). This doesn't have to be super-perfect, just as straight and neat as you can get it. Set the piping bag to one side: this will be used to pipe the pearl trim. Leave to set in the fridge.

~~~~~~~~

07. Repeat with the further two tiers. For a seamless look, keep the adjoining edges of each tier the same colour. So the middle tier should have a bottom ring colour that matches the top ring colour of the base tier, and the top ring colour will be the same as the base ring colour of the top tier.

~~~~~~~~

08. Once all of your cakes are neatly coated, pop them in the fridge for at least an hour to set.

~~~~~~~~

09. To assemble the cake, use cake dowels in the base tier and middle tier to prevent them collapsing. Use a little royal icing to secure each tier in place. (See pages 178–81 for dowelling technique.)

~~~~~~~~

10. To finish, place cake on a cake stand or an iced board. Using a No. 3 nozzle, pipe a trim around the base tier where the cake meets the stand or board, then pipe around base of the middle and top tiers in a matching colour (using buttercream that you have saved). Decorate with fresh flowers or a cake topper.

CHRISTMAS SNOWMEN MINI CAKES

These little cakes are an adorable twist on a traditional Christmas cake. Stand them proudly on the table as a group or give them away as presents (they are perfect for teachers). I have also used them as cake decorations on a very large Christmas cake, to create a snowman scene. As always, be creative and mix it up a bit by changing the decoration if you wish, e.g. adding sugar ear muffs or bobble hats. I like to give mine all funny expressions, and give the miserable one to Dad. Bah humbug! Rich fruit cake is moist and easy to shape, so the mini cakes are fun to make, especially with kids. If you don't like fruit cake, make them with the Belgian Chocolate Brownie Torte Cake (see page 209) – the version with Oreos in – popping the cake in a food processor to blitz it into crumbs and adding a little orange oil to the crumb mix to make it into chocolate orange cake. **Makes 5 snowmen**

STUFF YOU'LL NEED

Equipment:
> cake board
> pastry brush
> rolling pin
> impression rolling pin, impression mat or texture pin (optional – I used the Cake Boss pattern texture diamond rolling pin)
> small, sharp knife or ribbon cutter
> 4 cm (1½ in) small round cutter

The Cake:
> baked Rich Fruit Cake (see page 210), approx. 600 g (1 lb 5 oz), at room temperature

Ingredients:
> a little just-boiled apricot jam
> icing (confectioners') sugar, for dusting
> 600 g (1 lb 5 oz) natural marzipan
> vodka or cooled boiled water

> 1 kg (2 lb 3 oz) white sugarpaste
> a little stiff royal icing (see page 188 for recipe and consistency guide, or use shop-bought) in a piping bag
> 250 g (9 oz) packets of ready-coloured sugarpaste, in red, green, orange and black (or colour your own white sugarpaste with gel or paste colours)
> 1 tablespoon each of soft-peak

royal icing, coloured brown, in a piping bag with a No. 3 nozzle, and black, in a piping bag with a No. 3 nozzle

---

01. Start by making the fruit cake balls. Break up the fruit cake roughly and, for the large balls, squeeze approx. 80 g (3 oz) of the mixture together then roll between your palms (see pic 01 overleaf). It's like making Christmassy meatballs! For smaller balls, take about 35 g (1¼ oz) of fruitcake and do the same. Pop all of the balls – five large and five small – on a cake board and place in the freezer to firm up for about 30 minutes or in the fridge for 2 hours.

TIP › *To make rolling the fruit cake balls easier, have a bowl of warm water handy, and wet your hands in between rolling each ball.*

02. Brush each ball all over with a little apricot jam to make them sticky (see pic 02 overleaf).

TIP › *If you are making lots of these, it's quicker to rub the jam on your hands and roll the balls in your palms.*

03. Dust the work surface with icing sugar and roll out the marzipan to a thickness of 5 mm (¼ in). Cut the marzipan into pieces large enough to completely cover each of the large cake balls. Lay a marzipan piece over the top of each ball and press around the sides. Pick up a ball and pinch $\rightarrow$

underneath the base to gather up the excess marzipan. Trim this off (see pic 03). Roll the ball in your palms until smooth. Repeat with the remaining large and small balls. Place on a large cake board and leave them to dry overnight.

04. When ready to cover in icing, brush the balls with a little vodka or cooled boiled water, or use the palms of your hands to be super quick. Repeat Step 3 but use the white sugarpaste. If you see a little mark or crack where you have trimmed off excess icing, make sure this is on the underside so it won't show. Leave to dry for a few hours or overnight before decorating.

05. Take some stiff royal icing and dab a little on the top of each large ball to help the snowman heads stick onto the bodies (see pic 04). Place the small balls on top of the large ones.

06. Dust the work surface with icing sugar and roll out some red and green sugarpaste into two long strips. Keep it 4–5 mm (¼ in) thick so it doesn't break. If you want to add a pattern detail, use an impression pin or mat, rolling it with a firm pressure over the sugarpaste to emboss the pattern on the surface (see pic 05).

07. Cut out the scarves by using a small, sharp knife or ribbon cutter, about 5 cm (2 in) long and 1.5 cm (¾ in) wide (see pic 06). Pipe a little royal icing around the neck and down onto the body, and give the snowmen their warm, cuddly sugar scarves. Snip off the ends to make a nice, neat edge (see pic 07). Leftover sugarpaste can be stored in a sealed food bag.

07

08

09

08. For hats, roll out half of the black sugarpaste about 5 mm (¼ in) thick on a surface lightly dusted with icing sugar, and use the small round cutter or cut around something a similar size to create the bottom of the hats. Now roll out the remaining black sugarpaste into a sausage about 2 cm (¾ in) thick, cut into five chunks about 2 cm (¾ in) high then, using your fingers, narrow off the bottom and mould into a hat shape. Stick to the hat rims using a dab of royal icing. Attach the hats to the heads with another dab of royal icing (see pic 08).

TIP › *If you can see icing (confectioners') sugar on the cakes once you have finished, allow them to dry then brush off the excess with a dry pastry brush. For stubborn white spots, either spray with edible food lacquer (see page 224 for stockists) or use a brush dampened with vodka or cooled boiled water to remove. Ideally, dust as much icing sugar off the decorations as possible before applying them to the cake.*

09. Make carrot noses with a little orange sugarpaste. Shape small cones with your fingers and give them a twist to attach using a tiny dab of royal icing.

10. Use the brown soft-peak royal icing to pipe twiggy arms on the snowmen, as if they are holding their scarves down over their chubby tummies to keep out the cold.

11. Finally, add the eyes and mouth by piping little dots of black soft-peak royal icing (see pic 09). Leave the snowmen to dry overnight before displaying or boxing as gifts. Who can resist these jolly snowmen at Christmas time?

TOP TIP

Once the snowmen have set, they can be kept in a cake box for several weeks if you want to make them in advance of Christmas, or they can be individually boxed as gifts. (See page 224 for stockists of individual presentation bags and boxes.)

MEXICAN SKULL

I'm a big fan of Mexican EVERYTHING... I love the food, the style and the party vibe. This crazy Day of the Dead-style skull cake is a real showstopper and dead simple to make. To make the shape, I used a ready-shaped skull cake mould. Some people are a bit snobbish about using a shaped mould and prefer to carve and sculpt their cakes, but sometimes it's great to take a little shortcut, and this mould is really versatile (it can be used for pirate themes or Halloween, too). I used bright colours against a black base colour so it really 'pops', and used a build-up of simple flat sugar cut-outs with piping to bring out the edges around the coloured shapes and fill gaps.

STUFF YOU'LL NEED

Techniques:
> covering a shaped sponge
> simple cut-out fondant applique
> basic linea and pearl piping
> basic painting
> making moulded chocolate roses

Equipment:
> 3D skull mould (I used a Wilton Skull pan – see page 224 for stockists)
> bread knife or cake leveller
> palette knife
> pastry brush
> guide sticks

> large rolling pin
> small, sharp knife
> scriber needle or pin tool
> selection of large and small cutters (I used a mix of daisy, 5-petal, heart and single petal/teardrop shapes)
> paintbrush

The Cake:
> Vanilla Bean Sponge cake batter (see pages 200–202) to fill the mould (I used 2 kg/4 lb 6 oz batter, so it rose just above the top of the tin and could be cut down)

Ingredients:
> approx. 300 g (10½ oz) Vanilla Bean Buttercream (see page 216) and 2 tablespoons of strawberry jam, for sponge filling
> a little just-boiled apricot jam
> icing (confectioners') sugar, for dusting
> 1 kg (2 lb 3 oz) marzipan
> vodka or cooled boiled water
> 1 kg (2 lb 3 oz) black sugarpaste
> small handfuls of a selection of bright sugarpaste colours (I used lilac, orange, fuchsia, poppy red, pink, pastel yellow,

mint green, atlantic blue and baby blue)
> edible glue
> 1 tablespoon each of white and bright-coloured soft-peak royal icing, in a piping bag with a No. 2 nozzle (I used white, mint green, tangerine and pale yellow. See page 188 for recipe and consistency guide, or use shop-bought)
> ice blue dust colour
> 2 edible silver balls, for eyes
> red modelling-chocolate roses to decorate the table (optional, see pages 36–39)

01. Bake the cake in the mould cavities. Leave to cool, then cut down each sponge to the level of the tin, to make a flat surface.

02. Assemble the skull by adding a layer of buttercream to the cut side of one half, and a layer of jam on the other half, and sandwiching them together to create the 3D skull shape. Chill for an hour to set.

NOTE › *If you want to add more layers of flavour to the sponge, split each skull half and fill them with buttercream, before sandwiching the skull halves together (making 4 layers), although the skull shape might not be so neat.*

03. Brush the entire surface of the skull sponge with hot apricot jam using a pastry brush, then roll out the marzipan on a surface dusted with icing sugar, to guide-stick thickness. Remove the guide sticks and continue rolling out the marzipan until it is a few millimetres thinner: you want a thin coating so that the detail from the skull mould isn't lost. Carefully pick up the marzipan and drape it over the skull, smoothing it all over the sponge, avoiding air bubbles. Trim away the excess around the base and use your fingertips to press the coating against the sponge to bring out the teeth, eye sockets and jaw features etc. Leave to set overnight. →

04. The next day, lightly brush the marzipan layer with vodka or cooled boiled water and repeat the covering process with the black sugarpaste. Make sure there are no air bubbles (use a scriber needle or pin tool if you need to). Leave overnight to set.

05. Roll all your bright sugarpaste colours to a thin layer, and cut out colourful shapes. You can really make this design your own because it's so busy. For the yellow nose I chose a heart-shaped cutter. I then made sugar teeth with white sugarpaste, measuring the height of the teeth indentations and cutting pieces from a strip to create rounded-corner rectangles, and sticking them on with edible glue. For eyes I used a floral cutter shape and cut a circle from the centre to give me a floral white band around each socket. Add lots of different shapes to fill the front, top and side of the skull. I overlapped some large and smaller florals in different colours to add more detail.

06. Once you are happy with the shapes on your skull, pipe around some of the edges, add centres to the floral shapes, and finish the eyes. I used a touch of ice blue dust colour in the centre of the eye sockets on the white paste, to add streaks coming from within the eyes, and finished each eye with a small floral shape topped with a silver ball. Step back and see where there are spaces you need to fill. Pipe small tendrils and leaves in mint green with a No. 2 nozzle, and join up a few of the floral details to break up the mirror image. Leave to dry overnight.

07. To display the cake, place it directly on a table or a stand. I like to add a few sugar or chocolate roses around the base, so it looks even more authentic. The roses also hide the bottom of the cake where you cut away the excess icing, so the skull looks like it is floating on a bed of roses.

Make sure you keep the design symmetrical; if you add a heart shape to one cheek, do the same on the opposite in a mirror image. You can be more free-form with the piping fillers.

CHRISTMAS KITSCH COOKIES

I created these for a fun Harvey Nichols Christmas range one year, when 'ugly' festive jumpers were all the rage. They are great for a bit of camp Christmas fun, and make for a perfect edible gift, or tree decoration. The eye-catching argyle-style pattern is created using the flooding and marbling effect with royal icing, in which different coloured icings in lines are dragged through a base colour to create patterns. Alternatively, you can create 'flooded' designs with icing on a piece of greaseproof paper or plastic film sheet over a printed picture of your choice, tracing over it. Once it's set (after about two days), lift off the flooded royal icing picture and add it to the top of a cupcake or cake. The gingerbread lasts for several weeks if kept well wrapped. We sell these in cellophane bags tied with jolly Christmas ribbons. Makes approximately 16 cookies

STUFF YOU'LL NEED

Equipment:
› cocktail stick
› piping bags
› No. 2 nozzle and PME 13 star nozzle, or similar small star nozzle

The Cookies:
› 16 jumper-, mitten- and bobble hat-shaped baked cookies (I used Gingerbread Cookie Dough – see page 215). Use a shop-bought cutter or cut around a card template (see page 229)

Ingredients:
› 2 tablespoons soft-peak white royal icing, in a piping bag with a No. 2 nozzle (see page 188 for recipe and consistency guide, or use shop-bought)
› 250–300 g (9–10½ oz) each of runny royal icing in white, Christmas red and party green,

in plastic piping bags (see page 190 for royal icing consistency guide)
› 2 tablespoons stiff-peak white royal icing in a piping bag (you can also use red and green, for more variety) with a PME 13 star nozzle, or similar small star nozzle

---

01. Pipe a line of white soft-peak icing around the edge of each cookie shape, starting at the top, furthest away from you, and working towards the bottom of each cookie, lifting the piping bag up and allowing the icing to flow out slowly so that it falls around the edge, just within the shape (see pic 01 overleaf). Pipe in a continuous motion around each shape. Once you get back to the starting point, bring the nozzle towards the cookie and push the royal icing onto the starting point. Stop squeezing and pull the nozzle away. You may get a pointy bit sticking up when you do this if you are new to piping. It's not the end of the world, especially if you make sure your starting point is an area which you'll be piping over with the furry icing trim, but if you want to neaten it off use a small damp paintbrush to gently push down the little icing tail.

TIP › *If you are new to working with royal icing, practise on the work surface first so you can get the feel for piping.*

02. Once each shape is outlined, you can now 'flood' the inside of the shape with runnier icing (see pics 02 and 03 overleaf). Be creative and use different colours. To make polka-dot cookies, flood with one base colour, then, using a different icing colour, work above the cookie and allow little blobs to drop into the background colour. Space them out as equally as you can. Decorate one at a time, because if you leave the background colour for a few minutes, it will begin to 'skin over' so your cookies will look cracked when you drop in another colour. For stripy argyle-style cookies, flood the whole background colour, e.g. green, then drop over horizontal lines with red runny icing, then white to create stripes (see pic 04 overleaf). To create a marbled pattern effect, starting on one side of the cookie, sweep the cocktail stick through the runny icing in one motion, up and down in vertical lines through the horizontal lines, until you get to the other side of the cookie (see 05 overleaf). →

01

02

03

04

05

03. Once you've finished all the main flooded patterned parts, pipe stiff royal icing along the base of the hats and mittens to create the sugary fur trim and top the hats off with bobbles. Using a small star-shaped nozzle will create a ruffle effect (see pic 06). Begin on one side of the mitten or hat along the base and, using a firm and steady pressure, keeping the nozzle close to the cookie, pipe a slightly wavy line to fill up the bottom of the cookie. For the hat bobbles, pipe close into the cookie with a firm pressure to create a pompom effect, squeeze the icing in one spot until the bobble is the size you want. Leave to dry overnight and then wrap or serve as required.

06

christmas kitsch cookies / **125**

CLUB TROPICANA

I made a version of this cake for our 10-year wedding anniversary party. I had always wanted to make a spectacular cake, covered in tropical flowers but with no wires. I can't stand wired flowers, why not just use fresh? It looks impressive: really bright, and perfect for a summer theme party, and, as it's made of modelling chocolate, it tastes way better than sugarpaste. I love to make it with a Belgian Chocolate Brownie Torte (see page 209) as the cake, so it's like one of those Magnum lollies – dark chocolate in the middle with a white chocolate coating. You need to allow plenty of time for making all the flowers, but once they're made (you can do this a few weeks in advance and store them in cake boxes), assembling the cake is very quick. Serve with plenty of tropical cocktails and some cheesy 80s music to really set the scene!

STUFF YOU'LL NEED

Equipment:
› small rolling pin
› simple petal cutters – medium rose-petal cutter (approx. 4 cm/1½ in long), and large rose-petal cutter (approx. 4.5 cm/1¾ in long)
› lily veiner (for all the flowers), or husk from some corn on the cob to make vein-like impressions
› ball tool
› modelling tool
› small paintbrushes
› silver foil

› long leaf cutter
› fine cake tweezers
› silicone anthurium cutter and veiner
› pastry brush
› cocktail sticks

The Cakes:
› 10 cm (4 in), 18 cm (7 in) and 25 cm (10 in) round Belgian Chocolate Brownie Torte Cakes (see page 209), each baked in 2 tins, then split and filled and crumb-coated with chocolate buttercream, covered with

Belgian White Chocolate Paste (see page 223) or sugarpaste, and stacked with dowels to support (see pages 178–81)

Ingredients:
› icing (confectioners') sugar, for dusting
› 2 kg (4 lb 6 oz) white modelling chocolate (I use Squires Kitchen)
› paste colours, to dye the chocolate for flowers and leaves
› dust colours, to add depth to the flowers and their centres
› 200–250 g (7–9 oz) white

chocolate chips or broken bars
› double-thickness 40 cm (16 in) round cake board iced with sugarpaste (see pages 182–85) – I used ivory mixed with a little egg yellow
› rejuvenator spirit
› brown paste colour, for the painted inscription

THE FLOWERS

All the flowers are quite chunky. They are made from simple cut-out shapes, moulded by hand or with silicone veiners. Make 6–7 larger flowers and extra smaller, simpler filler flowers (the pink hibiscus and white frangipani-style chocolate flowers). Make all of the flowers in advance before assembling the cake, allowing them at least a day to set. If you are making the flowers on a hot summer's day, store them in the fridge. They might get a little condensation and go sticky, but they will dry out once stuck on the cake. Knead the paste colour into the Cocoform to dye it. For each colour, dye 300–400 g (10½–14 oz) of Cocoform (depending on what you want the most of). I used the following colours for the flowers:

PURPLE ORCHIDS: grape violet paste colour, with burgundy dust for detail.
RED STAR FLOWERS: Christmas red paste colour and dark brown
YELLOW LILIES: Yellow lilies: egg-yellow paste colour, with rust dust for detail.
PINK HIBISCUS: claret paste colour, with ruby dust for centres.
WHITE FRANGIPANI: no paste colour, just daffodil dust for centres.
WHITE & PINK ANEMONE: claret paste colour, with pink dust for petal edges .
GREEN & YELLOW ANTHURIUMS: bitter lemon/lime paste colour and egg yellow for the stamen, with apple-green dust for yellow stamen tips.
GREEN LEAVES: party green and spruce green paste colour, with moss dust for added detail. →

ORCHID CONSTRUCTION

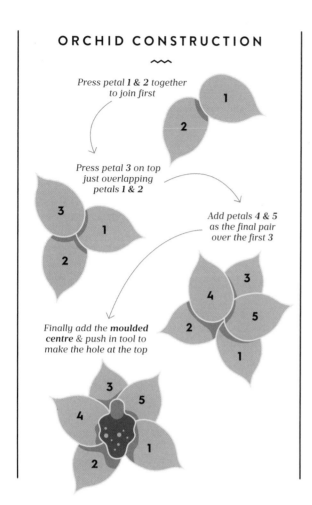

Press petal 1 & 2 together to join first

Press petal 3 on top just overlapping petals 1 & 2

Add petals 4 & 5 as the final pair over the first 3

*Finally add the **moulded centre** & push in tool to make the hole at the top*

PURPLE ORCHIDS

Roll out the purple Cocoform to a thickness of about 3–4 mm (if it's too thin, the chocolate flowers will flop and not hold their shape).

Take the medium rose-petal cutter and cut out five chunky petals. Press each petal into the lily veiner to flatten and thin out and add vein detail to each one.

Stick all of the petals together (see illustration opposite). Imagine the petals as if they are pointing like the hands on a clock. Start by securing the bottom two together pointing to 4 o'clock and 8 o'clock directions. Press together at the bases of each and squeeze between your fingers to join. Secure the third petal pointing up at 12 o'clock; press it firmly on top of the first pair. Finally add the fourth and fifth petals in a pair pointing to 2 o'clock and 10 o'clock. Lay these on top of the first 3 to make a 5-petal flower, then add the centre.

For the centre, take a small piece of purple Cocoform about the same size as a petal and make a cone. Flatten the cone and shape by hand to create the open-mouthed centre, then use a ball tool to press where the hole is and push it against all 5 petals. If you find the petals and centre fall open, make a round cup out of a strip of scrunched-up silver foil to sit the flower in, which will help to retain the shape until the Cocoform sets firmly.

PINK HIBISCUS

These are five-petal flowers. Make five small balls with the claret Cocoform. Flatten out each one to elongate it and make it into a long oval. Press out one of the ends to flatten. Repeat with the remaining ovals. Pinch in at the bottom point (which will be at the centre of the flower) and stand them next to each other. Squeeze the fat bits together to fuse them and dust the middle with ruby dust. Push into the middle with the end of a paintbrush or a pointed tool to accentuate the centre. Leave to set. These should hold their shape as they are smaller and the base of the cones act as a support.

YELLOW LILIES

These are two layers of three petals. Roll out the yellow Cocoform and cut 6 long lily petal shapes (I used a long leaf cutter). Use a veiner to add texture. Join three at the base of each one, roughly pointing to 12 o'clock, 4 o'clock and 8 o'clock. Do the same with next three petals and lay them on top of the first three, off-set so that you can see the petals behind the top layer. Use foil as a former to set.

For the centre, make a small trumpet/cone shape for the middle and then roll thin sausages of yellow paste to mimic the stamen and pollen bits you find in a lily. Paint with rust dust to give them that pollen-encrusted red tinge. Attach these with a little melted white chocolate and tweezers or steady fingers, once the large petals are stuck on the cake.

WHITE & PINK ANEMONE

Make these in the same way as the lilies, but with a larger rose-petal cutter and white Cocoform. Cut out 6 thick petals, add veining and secure in two layers of groups of three.

For the centres, roll some pink Cocoform into a ball, flatten and press onto the petals. Add impression holes with the pointed end of a modelling tool. Use foil to hold the shape if necessary. →

PURPLE
ORCHID

PINK
HIBISCUS

YELLOW
LILLIES

WHITE
& PINK
ANEMONE

WHITE
FRANGIPANI

GREEN &
YELLOW
ANTHURIUMS

RED STAR
FLOWERS

WHITE FRANGIPANI

Follow the method for pink hibiscus, using balls of white Cocoform, and dust their centres with yellow dust.

GREEN LEAVES

Roll out the green Cocoform slightly thinner than the petals. Cut several leaves out with the long leaf cutter and use a small rolling pin to elongate the leaves. Use the lily veiner or corn cob husk to add texture. Leave to set on a cake board. Make as many as you like, depending on how much leafy greenery you want to give your cake.

RED STAR FLOWERS

These are made of two layers of five petals. Roll out the red Cocoform following the purple orchid method on page 128, and cut out 10 petals with the same medium rose-petal cutter, marking veins with the lily veiner. Press the bottoms of the first five petals together to attach them, spacing them out evenly to create a basic five-petal shape. Do the same with the next five petals. Place the top five on the bottom five, off-set so that you can see the points of each petal poking out between the ones above.

For the centre, make a ball with a small piece of dark brown chocolate and flatten onto the flower. (You can make yellow centres if you prefer.) Make several impression holes in the centre with the pointed end of a modelling tool. Leave the flower to set, using scrunched-up foil to hold their shape, if necessary.

GREEN & YELLOW ANTHURIUMS

Roll out the lime Cocoform to a thickness of approx. 5 mm (¼ in) and use the anthurium cutter to cut out the shape. Press gently into the anthurium veiner. Leave to set in foil, making a little boat shape out of the foil to cradle the Cocoform so it will set into a rounded cup shape.

For the centres, roll sausages of yellow Cocoform and taper them off at one end. Dust the ends with green dust and leave to dry. Attach with a tiny bit of melted chocolate when you assemble the cake.

CHOCOLATE FANS

I made about 10 small and eight medium ruffled chocolate fans, to fill the tiers and for the top, using about 1 kg (2 lb 3 oz) of the Cocoform.

Roll out approx. 500 g (1 lb 2 oz) Cocoform to a 2–3 mm thickness, and cut it into 10–12 cm- (4–5 in-) wide lengths. Cut a straight line on the Cocoform and fold it back and forth in free-form fashion at about 1 cm (½ in) intervals; 4–5 folds is perfect (see above). Trim off the Cocoform and make a few more fans. To set them in a fan shape, turn the folded Cocoform on its side so the cut edges are upwards and pinch on one end. Open out the fan at the other end. Leave to set for at least 24 hours. →

TO DECORATE & ASSEMBLE THE CAKE

01. Melt the white chocolate in a microwaveable bowl or in a heatproof bowl set over a pan of just-simmering water (bain marie).

~~~~~~

02. Lay all your fans and flowers on the work surface. Brush the fans and flowers generously with melted white chocolate (using a pastry brush or spoon) and, starting on the base tier of the cake, press them against the cake

tiers, fitting them in where you can, like a flowery puzzle. If you find heavier flowers slip before the chocolate is set, secure them using a cocktail stick or two underneath, to take the weight. These can be removed once the chocolate has set hard.

~~~~~~

03. Once the base tier is covered, roll out a 20–25 cm (8–10 in) x 7 cm (3 in) strip of Cocoform (4–5mm/

¼ in thick) – you will need approx. 100 g (3½ oz). Pinch it together at either end to make creases and create a swag decoration. Spread melted chocolate all over the middle tier where you wish to attach the swag, and push it on. It will be heavy, so drape each pinched end over cocktail sticks while the chocolate sets. Build up flowers and fans around the swag detail, allowing some petals and leaves to creep over it. Push out either

side of the swag so that the detail stands out like a scroll on the cake tier. Continue all the way up the sides of the three tiers, right up onto the top tier. Place a few fans on the top to make a domed structure onto which to fix your chocolate flowers. Leave it to set for an hour before adding the final dust and painted details, and some of the flower centres.

~~~~~~~

04. Add the final details by mixing the dust colours with rejuvenator spirit and using a paintbrush to add dots and shading to the orchids, the lilies, the anemones and leaves. If you made the lily and anthurium centres, dip them in a little melted chocolate and hold them up to the middle of each flower with cake tweezers. Push them into the centres – they should hold,

but use a cocktail stick if you need to. Wipe away any chocolate that might be seen from the front with a clean dry paintbrush. Then use more dust if you need to, and finally add your inscription with a paintbrush (a fine No. 0 or 1 sable) with nutkin brown dust and rejuvenator spirit or neat dark brown paste colour as a paint, if you prefer.

STENCIL COWBOY CAKE

I first made a cake like this for a fun Wild West wedding photoshoot. Of course, you could make this cake for many parties, perhaps a kid's birthday or a barn dance-style event – it's fun, looks stunning and is pretty simple to create. I've used cowhide shapes for my stencils and an airbrush machine, but if you don't have an airbrush machine just paint with dust colours instead (still using the stencil). For extra detail, an impression mat gives the cake board a wood effect. The horns need a few days to dry, and your board and daisies need at least a day to set, so leave yourself plenty of time before assembling this design.

STUFF YOU'LL NEED

Equipment:
› 2 polystyrene cake dummies
› airbrush machine with edible brown liquid colour (or brown dust colour and rejuvenator spirit)
› small rolling pin
› pastry brush
› stitching tool wheel
› 35 cm (14 in) round cake board
› impression mat (see page 224 for stockists)
› daisy/marguerite plunger cutter
› foam or gel mat
› ball tool
› stencils (see page 229)

› scalpel
› 2 clean drawing pins or any pins (take great care not to lose any!)
› cake dowels
› gingham ribbon

The Cakes:
› 15 cm (6 in) and 23 cm (9 in) round cakes (any flavour sponge), iced in white sugarpaste (see pages 174–77)

Ingredients:
› approx. 300 g (10½ oz) petal paste for the horns, coloured with a little brown to make a

light brown base colour
› food lacquer or varnish (optional)
› approx. 50 g (2 oz) dark brown petal paste, for the leather trim on the horns (I used bulrush florist paste)
› vodka or cooled boiled water
› 1 tablespoon ivory soft-peak royal icing, in a piping bag with a No. 2 nozzle (see page 188 for recipe and consistency guide, or use shop-bought)
› sugarpaste for the board (I used 250 g/9 oz Renshaw chocolate brown, 250 g/9 oz teddy bear brown, and 250 g/9 oz ivory sugarpaste)

› icing (confectioners') sugar, for dusting
› approx. 30 g (1 oz) yellow petal paste (I used daffodil yellow)
› 1 tablespoon stiff-peak royal icing, for sticking
› 1 tablespoon brown soft-peak royal icing, in a piping bag with a No. 2 nozzle

01. Make the horns a few days in advance so they set hard. Roll out a fat sausage of the light brown petal paste and taper it off with your fingers at either end to make thinner horn ends. Lift up either side and create a pointed pair of horns (see pic 01 overleaf) and rest the ends of the horns on the two polystyrene cake dummies (or use some cling film-wrapped cookbooks).

When the horns are set, spray them brown, using the airbrush machine (or painting with dust colour mixed with rejuvenator spirit), followed by food lacquer or varnish if you wish, concentrating lots of colour on the tips to darken them.

Once the horns are completely dry, roll out the dark brown petal paste thinly and wrap it around the central part of the horns to create the 'leather' effect. Cut it to fit. Add a little vodka or cooled boiled water to stick the paste around the horns. Add detail using a stitching tool wheel along the edges of the brown leather (or create a dotted line using the end of a knife or scalpel by making little indentations). Finish the horns with cross-stitch-effect piping along the edges of the 'leather' and some dashes along the centre using a little soft-peak ivory royal icing. →

02. Cover the cake board at least a day in advance. Roll the sugarpaste (I used two browns and ivory) into three sausages and twist them together to create a marbled effect. Knead the paste until there are still a few subtle shades showing of each of the colours to add tone to your wood board. Dust the work surface with icing sugar and roll out and cover your board (see pages 182–85), then gently push the wood-effect impression mat into the icing (while the icing is fresh), to create the pattern (see pic 02). Lift up the mat and place it next to each previous impression until your board is covered.

~~~~~~~~~~

03. To make the yellow daisies, dust the work surface with icing sugar and roll out the yellow petal paste to a thickness of 2–3 mm. Cut out a daisy with the daisy cutter on the foam or gel mat, then push the shape out with the plunger mechanism. Press a ball tool gently on each petal from the outside towards the centre, to encourage each petal to curl up and give them some movement (see pic 03). Repeat until you have a few daisies, then leave these to dry out overnight, or make them up to a few weeks in advance.

~~~~~~~~~~

04. Make your cowhide stencils, drawing the shape on tracing paper, then marking it onto A4 card (or draw a few irregular free-hand shapes). Use a scalpel to neatly cut each shape out towards the lower part of the card, so that it will lay against the cake tier but the excess blank card will poke up above, making a screen and protecting the rest of the cake from the colour spray (see pic 04).

03

04

05

05. Spray the cowhide brown splodges around the white cake tiers (I do this before I stack them, to prevent too much spray going onto the upper or lower tiers, see pic 05). Use a drawing pin on each side of the stencils to hold them in place, taking care not to lose them. The tiny holes they make can be filled with a touch of white royal icing later (see page 192 on filling holes and cracks). Move around the cake, spraying (or painting) each shape, making sure you give yourself plenty of time. Leave each cowhide print to dry for 30 minutes, to avoid smearing previous wet prints. Leave the printed cakes to set, then stack the tiers onto your wood-effect base board with a little stiff white royal icing.

06. Add gingham ribbon around the base tier and top tier to cover the joins, then stick on the daisies with a small dab of royal icing on the back of each flower. Place them over the cake where you wish, then pipe on their brown centres. Attach your horns as the crowning glory, using stiff royal icing under the horns on the top of the cake to hold these in place. Yeeehaaaaw! Let's the party get started!

VINTAGE FLORAL PATCHWORK CAKE

This has got to be my favourite (if most challenging) way of decorating cakes. The idea for a cake with printed vintage fabric designs came to me one sleepless night, like a eureka moment. I knew a gorgeous English country garden-style wedding cake, inspired by the trend for vintage florals, would look amazing. I happened to meet Nikki of Francis-Dee, who came to see me as a bride for her wedding cake consultation. It turned out that she was a fabric designer. I told her all about my idea and she agreed to help by designing some lovely digital fabric prints. So, I made my first cake dummy, using printed icing paper. I took it to show the team at Wedding magazine – they were thrilled, as it was like nothing they'd ever seen before. And, as you can imagine, magazine editors LOVE a scoop. They set up a beautifully styled outdoor shoot, and the cake was revealed in the magazine in the summer of 2008, with Nikki credited for the fabric designs. My patchwork cake has inspired lots of ideas: I have since made print-wrapped 'tattoo cakes', cupcakes, cookies, chocolates and cake pops using edible prints. You can use the same technique with edible photos for birthdays, or to create a 'this is your life' cake (we made a fab one for Coronation Street's celebratory 50th anniversary). The possibilities are endless, and the world is your oyster once you get the hang of using edible print. The most important thing to remember about approaching this design is plan in advance and measure accurately, so that you have tiles that fit. You can find many ready-to-use prints or download prints from the internet (see stockists on page 224).

STUFF YOU'LL NEED

Equipment:
> 10 cm (4 in), 18 cm (7 in) and 2 x 25 cm (10 in) cake drums
> side scraper with measuring guide (or use the ruler)
> pastry brush
> rolling pin
> small, sharp knife
> cake smoothers
> royal icing rulers
> guide sticks
> palette knife or lifting tool
> piece of card
> pizza wheel cutter
> turntable (ideally a tilting turntable)
> piping bags with No. 2 and No. 3 nozzles
> spare bowl
> good-quality thick kitchen paper
> cake dowels

The Cakes:
> 10 cm (4 in), 18 cm (7 in) and 25 cm (10 in) square vanilla or fruit cakes (each cake made of 2 sponges, sandwiched with vanilla buttercream and strawberry jam – see pages 168–71). They should all be equal heights – ideally 8–10 cm (3–4 in) deep once split, filled and covered, so the cake looks in proportion

Ingredients:
> a little just-boiled apricot jam
> icing (confectioners') sugar, for dusting
> 3 kg (6 lb 10 oz) marzipan (or sugarpaste, if you don't want to use marzipan)
> 1 kg (2 lb 3 oz) white sugarpaste
> edible icing sheets (see page 224 for stockists, or create your own pattern and print it on edible paper) – for my 3 cm (1¼ in) tile size, I used 7 sheets of print, which gave me 48 tiles from each
> vodka or cooled boiled water
> 2 kg (4 lb 6 oz) stiff-peak royal icing (see page 188 for recipe and consistency guide, or use shop-bought)
> 15 cm (6 in), 20 cm (8 in) and double-height 35 cm (14 in) square cake drums, iced with ivory sugarpaste (see pages 182–85)

01

TOP TIP

~

When making a boxy design,
like this patchwork cake, it
makes a difference to the finish
if you panel the cake with
marzipan first (or sugarpaste if
you don't like marzipan), so that
the neat tiles will be perfectly
square and even.

02

03

04

05

06

07

08

COVERING THE CAKE IN MARZIPAN PANELS

01. Stick the largest filled sponge to a cake drum of the same size. Place this on a larger cake board and place the whole thing on top of a turntable. Crumb coat as per steps on pages 170–71 or see pic 01. Coat the cake with a layer of apricot jam (see pic 02).

02. Dust the work surface with icing sugar and roll out a long piece of marzipan about 2.5 cm (1 in) wider than the width of the drum, then elongate to make one long rectangular strip (see pics 03 and 04). For example, if you are covering an 18 cm (7 in) square x 10 cm (4 in) high cake on its drum, you want to roll out a rectangle approx. 20 cm (8 in) x 46 cm (18 in).

03. Place a spare drum (the same size as the sponge) on the marzipan and use it as a template. Cut around the drum, then lift the marzipan carefully and place it on top of the cake (see pic 05). Line up the panel so it is aligned with the cake and push it on gently with a smoother. Add more jam all around the cut edge of the marzipan on the top of the cake (see pic 06).

04. Now, cut out a piece of marzipan for the first side. You know it's 18 cm (7 in) across, so cut around the drum but, using a ruler as a guide, cut the piece just over 10 cm (4 in) wide, so that it measures approx. 18 cm (7 in) long and just over 10 cm (4 in) deep. Lift it up to one side of the cake and line it up neatly along the base. It should fit neatly up to the top panel. Use a side smoother to push it against the side and top of marzipan (see pic 07). If you think it is not level or too high, cut along the top edge at a 90-degree angle with a small, sharp knife, to trim away any excess and leave you with a sharp edge. Add a little jam to the edges of the marzipan panels on the first side.

05. Next add the further three sides, bearing in mind that the next side is now the width of the cake, but with an additional few millimetres from the panel of marzipan on the first side, so use the cake drum as a guide to cut, but for the third side, shift the drum over a few millimetres, to allow for the thickness of the marzipan, cutting it a little wider. Lift up piece three and attach it to the cake in the same way. Continue all the way around, bearing in mind that the fourth side will also be a little wider to allow for the two marzipan panels it will be covering (see pic 08). Once everything is covered, use a clean side smoother to push everything nice and square. Repeat this method with the two smaller cake tiers. Leave to dry overnight on a spare cake drum.→

MAKE THE SUGAR TILES

Before You Start:

〜〜〜

Measure the height of your sponges (including the drum underneath). You need to plan this in advance so you know your tiles will fit (though if the worst comes to the worst you can cut tiles in half and use these at the corners of the tiers). Divide the cake height by three (if you want rows of three, as pictured) and work out the size you'll be cutting your tiles to. For instance, if your cake measures 9 cm (3½ in) high, cut your tiles into 3 cm (1¼ in) squares.

Measure the side of each cake tier across the width, and multiply this by four. This will give you the total length you need to cover (you need three rows to cover the height). So for example, if you've made 3 cm (1¼ in) tiles and your top tier is about 12 cm (5 in) wide, you'll need four tiles per row x 3 tiles high for each of the four sides of the cake. Allow for the tops, too.

Calculate the number of tiles you need to cover the exposed surfaces of the cake. For this three-tier cake I used about 300 tiles (making extra in case of breakages). This sounds like a lot but they're quick to make once you've rolled out the sugarpaste.

Make the tiles a few days in advance (at least 24 hours), so they have time to dry before you apply them to the cake, and give yourself plenty of time to cut them out (so that all the tiles are the same size). They have a long shelf-life.

01.

01. Dust the work surface with icing sugar and roll out a 250 g (9 oz) piece of sugarpaste in a rectangular shape (at least A4 size, to fit your edible paper) to guide-stick thickness, rolling out from the centre and away from you, turning the sugarpaste periodically, so that the sides are straight, then remove the guide sticks and roll it thinner, to a thickness of 1–2 mm – you should be able to fit 2 x A4 edible sheets onto the icing. Keep sweeping plenty of icing sugar underneath the sugarpaste as you roll, so that when you stick the edible sheet on the icing, it won't stick to the work surface. The sheets are delicate and tear very easily.

〜〜〜〜〜〜

02. Take one of the edible printed sheets, release it carefully from its backing using a palette knife, and leave it to one side while you brush the sugarpaste sheet all over with a little vodka or cooled boiled water (don't over-wet it or your images will start to dissolve).

TOP TIP

~

Use two royal icing rulers, if you have them, to keep the sugarpaste an equal thickness, as you would with regular guide sticks. You can then roll to the depth of the icing rulers, or substitute with regular rulers, which will prevent you from rolling out icing that's thicker in one place than another, giving you different tile thicknesses.

Carefully lay the sheet on the damp sugarpaste, taking care to ensure there are no trapped air bubbles. Smooth over gently with your fingers.

~~~~~~

03. Cut out the tiles in a grid, before the sugarpaste dries. I used a strip of card cut to the size I needed as a guide (see picture 03, above left), to make sure all the tiles are the same size. Line the card right up to the edge of the printed sheet, hold down the card with a ruler (not too hard – you don't want to dent the sugarpaste), and carefully slice along the straight line where the image finishes with a pizza wheel cutter (see pic 01).

~~~~~~

04. Keeping the card in place, cut along the length of the other side of the card. This gives you one long strip in the correct width. Continue cutting all the way across your sheet, using the last cut side as your next point to line your card up to, and cut another line down the width of your strip. Once you have finished cutting these few lines, you will have 4 or 5 strips of patterned sugarpaste. Carefully repeat the process across the horizontal to create your square sugar tiles. Once you have finished, carefully lift each tile and pop it onto spare square cake boards (dusted with a little icing sugar) to dry out. Continue until you have enough tiles for your cake. Leave the tiles to set in a cool, dry and ventilated place (not in an airtight container) for at least 24 hours. $\rightarrow$

01

02

TOP TIP

~~~

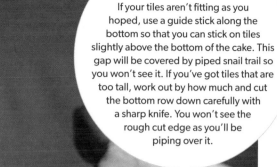

If your tiles aren't fitting as you hoped, use a guide stick along the bottom so that you can stick on tiles slightly above the bottom of the cake. This gap will be covered by piped snail trail so you won't see it. If you've got tiles that are too tall, work out by how much and cut the bottom row down carefully with a sharp knife. You won't see the rough cut edge as you'll be piping over it.

03

04

05

BUILD THE CAKE

01. Put your first cake onto the turntable. Line up the tiles along one side of your cake, roughly spacing them out before sticking them on, so you can see if you need to space them out a bit more, and avoid having to use cut tiles at any ends (see pic 01). You need the tiles to finish just under the edge of the top, so you have space to pipe a trail along the cake's edges to finish.

02. Pipe the stiff royal icing with a No. 3 nozzle along the bottom edge of the first side. This is your base for the grid of tiles. Fix the tiles to the cake by pressing them gently into the icing, then start building up the rows (see pic 02). Set them closely together, with equal space between each row, so that you don't have really thick grouted lines between the tiles. If you need to, leave a gap at each corner which can be covered with 'snail trail' piping. When you have completed a line, take a cake smoother and push it gently along the cake edge to level all the tiles, so the surface of the cake is flush and neat (see pic 03). Continue fixing tiles until the side is complete, making the tiles neat with a side smoother. Spin the cake around and start on the next side. Continue until you have all four sides covered.

03. Whether you are making a single tier or a multi-tier cake you will need to decorate the top with tiles. Lay out all your tiles in a grid to get the spacing right (you don't want half pieces or wonky lines), then fix each tile with royal icing. Use a top smoother at the end to encourage all the tiles to be level. Leave the cake to set overnight.

04. The tile grouting is my favourite and most satisfying part of the project, as it transforms the cake. You will need about 1 kg (2 lb 3 oz) of the stiff-peak royal icing for a three-tier cake. Stick each square cake onto its iced cake drum, making sure the cakes are central. Fill a piping bag (fitted with a No. 2 or No. 3 nozzle, depending on how much of a gap you have between your tiles) with royal icing. Start off piping between each row of tiles on the vertical column down one side of your cake, carefully pushing just enough between the tiles to fill the gap between each column (see pic 04). Once you have filled all the vertical lines, go across horizontally to fill the gap between each row.

After you have filled all the spaces, drag a clean finger across each line to smooth off the excess icing. Continue piping between rows until your entire cake is grouted.

TIP › *Have a bowl of water sitting next to you to rinse off the sticky icing that builds up on your fingers, and some kitchen roll for drying. If you get icing on the patterned tiles, carefully wipe it off straight away with a damp (not wet) piece of kitchen roll.*

05. Once your cake is grouted, fill a piping bag (fitted with a No. 3 nozzle) with royal icing and pipe a 'snail trail' down each corner's edge (see pic 05 and detailed instructions on page 193). Ideally, you need a tilting turntable so that you can lift the cake to an angle for piping. If not, prop up your cake at the edge on a few spare cake boards or a big cookbook. When you have piped down the corners, pipe a 'trail' around the bottom of the cakes where they join the boards. Pick the side of the cake you like the best to be the front, then begin in the middle of the back in one direction and pipe all around the base tier until you get back to the starting point. Finally, to finish your spectacular creation, repeat the 'trail' along the top edge of each tier to pipe a trail of icing pearls to finish the edge. Top with fresh flowers. Beautiful!

DOWELS

This cake is stacked with dowels in the same way as other stacked cakes, but there is an additional iced board under each cake, so just place each one on top of the tier below (see pages 178–81). It's a good cake for taking to a venue in three separate tiers, as you just stack them on the table rather than having to glue them together in a one-piece construction.

WOODLAND CREATURES FONDANT CUPCAKES

These fun and simple cupcakes appeal to children and adults alike, and are playful in design, so just have fun! I went for a folksy feel for the little creatures and used autumnal colours for the fondant. The creatures are made of sugarpaste cut-outs, with hand painting and soft-peak royal icing for details. I have lots of cutters that I've accumulated over the years, but if you don't you can mould these tiny critters by hand. Fill your cupcake cases with sponge mixture just halfway: this gives them a good rise to the top, leaving enough room for the icing. If you find the tops have a large hump and your fondant won't sit flat, just trim the sponge down. **Makes approximately 12–16 cupcakes**

STUFF YOU'LL NEED

Equipment:
› small rolling pin
› guide sticks
› small round cutters in various sizes, plunger style or regular
› small paintbrush
› small, sharp knife or ribbon cutter
› 2 x piping bags fitted with No. 2 nozzles
› small rose-leaf plunger cutter
› small, sharp scissors
› Dresden and bone tool

› tiny blossom plunger
› small heart-shaped plunger cutter
› 3 x bowls
› 3 x desssert spoons
› pin tool or cocktail stick

The Cupcakes:
› 8–12 baked cupcakes (I prefer vanilla, lemon or orange sponge under fondant – it doesn't sit well on a chocolate one and the flavours don't really go together)

Ingredients:
For the woodland creatures:
› icing (confectioners') sugar, for dusting
› coloured sugarpaste, 40 g (1½ oz) of each colour
› edible glue or cooled boiled water
› 50 g (2 oz) each soft-peak royal icing (see page 188 for recipe and consistency guide, or use shop-bought), coloured black and white

For the cupcakes:
› 500 g (1 lb 2 oz) pack fondant icing sugar (enough to cover 12–16 muffin-sized cupcakes)
› 3 tablespoons boiled water (still warm)
› paste colours (I used autumn leaf, dark brown and gooseberry)

WOODLAND CREATURES COLOURS

〜〜

BADGER: black, ivory / **FOX:** orange & brown mix to make rust, ivory, black / **HEDGEHOG:** powder blue, & the racoon body colour for his face / **RACOON:** yellow & ivory mix / **BUNNY:** teddy-bear brown, ivory & pink mix / **MUSHROOM:** chocolate brown & poppy mix (I also used this for other creatures' facial details & paws), powder blue, ivory / **SQUIRREL:** I mixed some of bunny & raccoon colours together to make these / **OWL:** ice blue, mint green & white

01. Start by making your woodland creatures. You can do this the day before, or even a few weeks in advance.

All the creatures except the squirrel and mushroom start off from a 4 cm (1½ in) round cut-out shape as the main body. Use edible glue or water to stick the bits together if you need to, but most stick naturally when freshly cut and moulded. →

FOR THE BADGER: Roll out the black sugarpaste to guide-stick thickness and cut out the 4 cm (1½ in) body circle. Cut an additional circle for the face but move the cutter over the shape and cut it down to a squashed oval by cutting a bit away. Stick the face on the body in-line with the top of the body. Mould two blobs for ears and stick them on with your brush and edible glue (or water), and do the same with a small sausage for the tail. Roll out a very thin piece of ivory sugarpaste and cut two thin strips with a sharp knife or ribbon cutter for the face detail. Stick on the strips and trim off any excess. Pipe a small strip of white icing around the bottom. Add a tiny ball of black sugarpaste for his nose and pipe the eyes with black royal icing first then pipe over with white to finish.

FOR THE FOX: Roll out the rust-coloured sugarpaste to guide-stick thickness and cut out the 4 cm (1½ in) body circle. Cut out little ears with the end of the rose-leaf plunger cutter and two feet with a tiny polka-dot plunger (or just make two small balls and flatten them). Roll a sausage and form into a cone-like swirl for the tail; for the nose make a small cone for his face in the same colour. Stick these all together to make the main body. Roll out a little white sugarpaste and use the leaf cutter to make the chest part and two tiny cut circles for his eyes (or two small flattened balls) and add a tiny piece of white sugarpaste for the tip of the tail and ears. Stick these on. Finish by adding a tiny ball of black for the nose and tiny balls of black for the eyes, then pipe white on the eyes and pipe white claws.

FOR THE HEDGEHOG: Roll out the powder-blue sugarpaste to guide-stick thickness and cut out the 4 cm (1½ in) body circle. Elongate it slightly and pinch at one end to make his nose. Use a small pair of scissors to make little cuts around the body for spikes, then make small indentations with the tip of a sharp knife. Mould tiny pieces of yellow sugarpaste from the racoon colour for the face and add two tiny balls of sugarpaste from the mushroom colour for the little eye and nose. Make a small cut for the mouth and stick on two tiny balls for the paw.

FOR THE RACOON: Follow the method for making the badger body and head using the yellow and ivory mix, then add a moulded curly tail. Make the ears in the same way as the fox. For the eyes, roll a tiny bit of mushroom-colour sugarpaste and cut a tiny circle in half for each eye marking. Use little balls of the same colour for the nose and feet. Pipe the eyes with white royal icing. I hand-painted the stripy tail, the inside of the ears and dots on the eyes with dark brown and neat chestnut paste colour on a small brush.

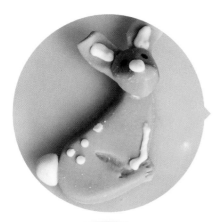

FOR THE BUNNY: Roll out the teddy-bear brown sugarpaste to guide-stick thickness and cut out the bunny shape with a small knife. Smooth the body and add leg detail using a modelling tool, making an impression for the leg and marks for the claws. For the head, add a small piece of moulded sugarpaste in a teardrop shape and add ears by making two flattened sausages of sugarpaste. Add two tiny pieces of ivory sugarpaste to the ears, add a tiny ball for the nose and a small ball for the tail. Pipe dots of white royal icing onto its back and a line down its stomach. Use the paintbrush from the eyes to finish.

FOR THE MUSHROOM: Roll out the brown sugarpaste to guide-stick thickness and cut out the 4 cm (1½ in) body circle. Cut away the bottom of the circle with the same cutter to make a mushroom shape. I used a little of the hedgehog's pale blue to hand-mould the stalk, then added dots using tiny flattened blobs of ivory sugarpaste.

NOTE

Leave all of your creatures on a spare cake board to set (overnight, or leave them several weeks), then once your cupcakes are iced and set you can apply them with a tiny bit of royal icing.

FOR THE SQUIRREL: Roll out the mixed sugarpaste to guide-stick thickness and cut out the 4 cm (1½ in) body circle. Elongate it to a pear shape. I used a spare angel-wing cookie cutter to make the tail, but you can mould or cut it any way you like to add a bushy tail up and around the main body. For the face, use a ball made into a cone or teardrop and add tiny ears, hand-moulded in a pinch on each side of the head. Paint the eyes, ears and tail details with the same brush from the racoon and bunny. Make the feet with mushroom sugarpaste, rolled and cut out with a tiny blossom plunger; two cut in half to make four feet. For his tummy, cut out a heart-shaped piece of thinly rolled ivory paste.

FOR THE OWL: Roll out the turquoise colour sugarpaste and cut out the 4 cm (1½ in) body circle and cut a small 'V' indentation in the top to shape the head. With the excess cut away part, roll this tiny bit a bit thinner and cut out with the tip of a leaf cutter if you have one (or just cut in half and use a knife for markings) and then half this piece to create his wings. For creating his big wide eyes cut out little circles from some yellow, thin sugarpaste and smaller circles from the mushroom colour and pop these in place. Finish the details with some of the white royal icing to add pupils, wavy lines on his chest and add a tiny bit of hand moulded rust colour sugarpaste for his beak and feet. →

ICING THE CUPCAKES

01.Place the fondant icing sugar into a bowl and stir in a few splashes of warm water. Take care, as you want it to be just the right consistency, not so runny that the icing won't set, but not so stiff that it won't drop off the spoon – you are looking for a treacle-like consistency, so it clings to the spoon but will drop off it if it's held aloft. Stir slowly until you have the right smooth consistency with no dry sugary bits. Split the mixture between two more bowls (a third in each) to make the separate colours.

02.Add colouring a little by little to the 3 bowls (using separate metal dessertspoons) until you are happy with the shade.

NOTE › *The coloured icing will look slightly darker when it sets. Paste colours are very strong so you only need a tiny amount to dye the fondant. Cover the bowls with damp cloths (see TOP TIP).*

03.Take a clean dessertspoon and slowly spoon the fondant onto the middle of your cupcake. The liquid fondant will slowly start to spread towards the edges of the case, and you should be able to tell if you need to add a little more (see pics 01 and 02). Work quickly, as it sets fast and begins to 'skin over' when exposed to the air. If you have too much, invert the cupcake back over the bowl (avoid letting crumbs of cake get into the bowl of icing), and tip upright once some of the fondant has dripped away. To encourage the fondant to settle flat on the cakes gently tap them on the work surface until the icing has flooded the case.

04.Check the finish and if you notice tiny bubbles appearing in the icing, pop them with your pin tool or a cocktail stick, then tap it again to flatten the icing (see pic 03). Leave to set for 24 hours until the icing is set hard, then top with the woodland decorations. They should stick pretty well, but add a tiny dab of royal icing or use edible glue to stick them on if you need to. The iced and decorated cupcakes will keep for up to five days.

OWL

MUSHROOM

FOX

BADGER

BLACK SOFT-PEAK
ROYAL ICING

BUNNY

HEDGEHOG

WHITE SOFT-PEAK
ROYAL ICING

RACOON

SQUIRREL

TOP TIP

Lay a damp cloth over
each bowl of icing as soon
as you have made it and
coloured it – liquid fondant
'skins over' quickly and
this will result in a
messy finish.

MULTI-CHOCOLATE ROSE CAKE

This cake is gorgeous for so many reasons: it tastes amazing as it's covered with Belgian chocolate flowers; it's extremely quick to assemble (once you've made all of the roses!); and it works in any colour scheme. This lavender, lilac, peaches and vintage-pink mini 3-tier version was inspired by the beautiful wedding cake I made for Fearne Cotton (Fearne's was a huge 5-tier cake with OVER 700 roses!). Once it's encrusted with roses, it looks much bigger and is a perfect size for a small wedding (it will serve about 60 lucky guests). For this cake, you need to make about 250 roses, depending on their size.

STUFF YOU'LL NEED

Equipment:
> pastry brush or spoon
> cocktail sticks
> 6 x cake drums (see note)
> lilac or cream ribbon, enough to cover the base cake drum

The Cakes:
> 10 cm (4 in), 15 cm (6 in) and 20 cm (8 in) round Belgian Chocolate Brownie Torte Cakes (see page 209, each tier is made up of 2 sponges)

Ingredients:
> 200–250 chocolate roses made with approx. 3 kg (6 lb 10 oz) Cocoform modelling chocolate (see pages 36–39). I made mine with grape violet, navy, claret, baby blue, mint and tangerine
> approx. 100 pale-green chocolate leaves (I used gooseberry paste colour) made with a rose-leaf plunger cutter (see page 75)
> 1.5 kg (3 lb 5 oz) Belgian White Chocolate Roll-Out Paste (see page 223) (roll thin as it will be covered with chocolate roses)
> 750 g (9 oz) white chocolate chips, or broken bars

NOTE › *The cake drums are stacked together to make 1 double-thickness drum and iced with lilac sugarpaste (see pages 178–81) and wrapped in ribbon. You will need:*

2 x 10 cm (4 in) cake drums
2 x 15 cm (6 in) cake drums
2 x 40 cm (16 in) cake drums, iced (I used a lilac sugarpaste)

01. Make all the chocolate roses in advance (a few weeks ahead if you wish) and keep them laid out on cake boards inside cake boxes. If leaving for more than two weeks, wrap a loose layer of cling film around the cake boards to stop the roses from drying out. Make the leaves and leave to set on a spare cake board.

~~~~~~~

02. To assemble the cake, split, fill and crumb-coat the cakes with the chocolate buttercream (see pages 168–71), then cover the cakes with Belgian White Chocolate Roll-Out Paste (same technique as on pages 174–77). Stack the cakes on the iced cake board using dowels (see pages 178–81)

with the middle tier cake sat on the two 15 cm (6 in) cake boards and the top tier cake sat on the two 10 cm (4 in) cake boards, to give the cakes extra height and support.

03. Melt the white chocolate in a bowl or in a heatproof bowl set over a pan of just-simmering water (bain marie). Brush the base of a rose with the chocolate and, starting at the bottom, stick the roses to the cake, tucking in little leaves between the gaps as you go, using a little chocolate on the bottom of the leaves to adhere. Take care not to get chocolate on the board or on the front of any flowers. Arrange them in single colours or groups of three of one colour (see pics 01 and 02 overleaf).

~~~~~~~

04. Continue sticking roses and leaves all the way up the cake tiers (see pic 03 overleaf). If you find some chocolate roses are heavy, use a cocktail stick under the roses to support them while the chocolate dries (see pic 04 overleaf). Cover all the tiers and leave to set for a few hours. Wrap the base board with ribbon to finish. →

01

02

TOP TIP
~~
Using double ribboned caked drums inbetween each tier gives more height.

03

04

SECTION THREE

THE BASICS

*All the info you'll need for making
your own Cake Projects*

TECHNICAL JARGON

Like any hobby or trade, there are a few specialist terms in the cake-making industry that could do with being demystified. If in doubt, you can always turn to the internet. I might sound a bit old here, but when I first started getting into cakes, we didn't have online support like YouTube, but now you can find hundreds of tutorials.

ACETATE PAPER

A clear, plastic, flexible paper that can be used for creating run-outs. As it is translucent you can trace images through it. Alternatively, use plastic stationery document wallets or white baking parchment.

BAKING PARCHMENT

A thick, moisture- and grease-proof paper used to line baking tins and trays. It can be used to make piping bags, too.

BLEEDING

When one icing runs or spreads into another. A lighter colour icing can get stained by a stronger shade, especially on run-outs or cookies decorated with royal icing. It can also happen when two shades of sugarpaste are used (particularly if there is a lot of humidity in the atmosphere).

BLOOM

When chocolate develops white patches (when the cocoa butter or sugar crystals rise to the surface). It might spoil the look, but it won't change the taste.

BRUSH EMBROIDERY

A decorating technique where a piped royal icing pattern outline is brushed inwards with a soft damp brush to create an embroidered effect. I've used this on my Vase & Flowers cake (see page 26).

CAKE LACE

An edible liquid paste that can be used in sheets or strips by pushing into a silicone lace mould mat. The liquid sets firmly and can then be peeled from the mould to give you large strips of edible lace. Some old-school cake decorators do not like these, as it takes away the need to be able to pipe perfectly by hand with royal icing. It's a foolproof way to add amazing detail to cakes without requiring piping skills.

CRUMB COATING/DIRTY ICING

A thin layer of buttercream that seals the sponge layers to keep in the crumbs and fill any small gaps, holes or snags.

CRUST OR SKIN OVER

A term used to describe when the surface of your icing or royal icing run-outs start to dry and form a hard crust on the surface. This prevents one colour staining another, and in cake decorating you often have to wait for this to happen before moving on to the next step.

EDIBLE GLITTER

You can get this in countless shades. I particularly like the Rainbow Dust.

EDIBLE-INK CARTRIDGES

Cartridges filled with edible ink (food colouring), which can be used with a normal printer but the printer must be used for edible ink purposes only.

EDIBLE-INK PEN

These resemble felt tips but are made with food colouring instead. Genius things!

EDIBLE SUGAR SHEETS

Edible paper or frosting sheets made primarily of cornstarch, corn syrup or sugar. As well as being used in edible-ink printers to produce edible pictures and patterns, it can be airbrushed or cut into shapes. I love it and use it in the Vintage Floral Patchwork Cake (see page 139), Doggy Biscuits (see page 104) and Not-So-Dirty Burger (see page 79).

FLOODING

When you fill in a section of outlined royal icing with a more liquid royal icing colour, to make blocks or shapes of colour to decorate a cookie or cake.

FOOD LACQUER OR SHELLAC SPRAY

Edible spray used to add a shine to decorations. I use it on my Monochrome Chevron Cake (see page 45), to make the chocolate jewellery look more plastic fantastic.

FORMERS

These are solid plastic forms or shapes used to dry sugar flowers, leaves or other pieces. You can make your own using sugarpaste under cling film, or use folded card. I've used some tin foil as a former to support my large tropical flowers in my Club Tropicana project (see page 127).

GANACHE

A mixture of chocolate and cream, used for filling or covering a cake.

GEL COLOUR

A strong food colouring in gel form. It is less runny than a liquid colour but not as intense as a paste. It's good for using in buttercreams or liquids such as royal icing or piping gels.

GLITTERISING

When you apply non-toxic glitter to the surface of a cake, cookie or sugar decoration to add magical sparkliness.

GLYCERINE

A sweet, odourless syrup and softening agent, which can be added to royal icing or fondant to soften it. It can also be mixed with melted chocolate to thicken it for piping work or to make modelling chocolate.

GUIDE STICKS (OR MARZIPAN SPACERS)

You can buy these from sugarcraft suppliers; they are used to ensure an even thickness when you roll out sugarpaste, marzipan, chocolate coatings or cookie dough.

GUM ARABIC

When gum arabic is mixed with water, it can be used as a glaze for marzipan, or as edible glue for sugarpaste. Used as a glaze, it gives the decoration a glossy sheen.

GUM TRAGACANTH

This is a plant-derived product that can be used to stiffen sugarpaste and will make it set harder and hold its shape. It is particularly handy for modelling, when you need shapes to stay in form.

LEVELLING

To make your cake or icing level on the surface.

LIQUID GLUCOSE

A viscous sugar solution of glucose suspended in liquid, which is sold in jars or tubs. You can find it in the baking section of supermarkets, from chemists, or from chocolate and baking suppliers. We use it when we make our chocolate paste, as when it's added to chocolate it enables it to be moulded or rolled out.

LUSTRE (OR DUST COLOURS)

Lustre dusts are non-toxic powders. Mixed into vodka or cocoa butter, they can be painted directly on sugar decorations or the cake itself. They can also be applied as they are, with a dry brush. There are many different colourful and metallic lustres, which can be used on sugar flowers, embellishments or iced surfaces to give them a twinkling, metallic effect.

LUSTRE SPRAY

An edible spray that can be used to decorate and add sheen to a cake's surface or to sugar decorations, giving them a metallic shine. It is quicker than painting on lustre dust.

MARBLING

When two or more colours of icing are added to a base coat of royal icing, then a toothpick is dragged through it to create a swirly, patterned effect. (See Christmas Kitsch Cookies on page 122.) Or multiple colours of sugarpaste that are kneaded together but not properly mixed.

METALLIC PAINT

Ready-made metallic paint, often available as paint 'pens'. The Rainbow Dust brand is one of my favourites. I use them to create edible bugs for the Framed Insect Taxidermy cakes (see page 50).

PALETTE KNIFE

A tool for spreading and smoothing fillings or icings. They come in a range of sizes.

PASTE COLOURING

Professional, strong, cake-decorating colourings that have the advantage of not affecting the consistency of sugarpaste or liquid icings, as liquid food colourings can. →

PEARLS

Small, round piped dots of royal icing.

PETAL PASTE (OR FLORIST PASTE)

A stiff sugarpaste used for making flowers. It can be rolled very thinly and sets rock-hard, so petals look less chunky and more realistic. It dries out very quickly. I prefer the Squires Kitchen brand.

PIPING

When you force royal icing, chocolate icing or buttercream through a nozzle (or straight from a piping bag), to create a message, add detail or texturise a cake.

PIPING BAG (OR PASTRY BAG)

Cone-shaped plastic, fabric or paper bags, used by themselves or with piping nozzles inserted, for piping chocolate, royal icing and buttercream. You can make your own with baking parchment (see page 166).

PIPING GEL

A clear sugar-based gel, used for giving a cake's surface a water/ripple effect, or a jewel effect. You can add colour or edible glitters. It holds its shape and sets firm.

PIPING NOZZLES, TUBES OR TIPS

Used for piping lines, swirls, flowers, patterns and messages onto cakes with royal icing or buttercream. You can get loads of different shapes and sizes such as circle, star or leaf tip openings. Ideally use those made of stainless steel, not plastic.

PLUNGER CUTTER

A cake-decorating tool that cuts out then ejects a shape.

PRESSURE PIPING

A piping technique that uses varying amounts of pressure through the nozzle of a piping bag, to create a more shaped piping design, with thicker parts that trail off to thinner parts, and vice versa.

REJUVENATOR SPIRIT (OR RJ SPIRIT)

A food-grade alcohol used to dilute lustre dusts, tints and blossom tints and create edible paints. It's great for gold, pearls, metallics or silver paint effects. Because it has a very high alcohol content it evaporates quickly and will not make your cake or decorations too wet.

ROLLED FONDANT (OR REGALICE)

See sugarpaste entry.

ROYAL ICING

The cake decorator's cement! A white or coloured liquid icing made with icing sugar, egg white and lemon juice, that sets hard. You can add glycerine to it to keep it softer and easier to cut through. It's used for piping decorations and writing messages, as well as fixing and sticking cakes together. It's an essential for cake decorating if you want to make iced cakes and make them look more professional, but is a fairly old-fashioned method of cake covering (rolled pastes are more commonly used nowadays). See page 188 for recipe, consistency guide and techniques.

RUN-OUT

A shape or decoration made with royal icing. Also known as 'flood work', it involves piping runny royal icing onto parchment paper or acetate paper, or directly onto the surface of a cookie or cake, within an outline. When the shape dries, you have an icing design which you can use for all kinds of decorating for cakes, cookies and cupcakes.

SANDING SUGAR

A large, granular sugar that comes in many colours and is used for cookie decorating or cake decorating. It creates a sparkly look.

SCORING

Making a mark or scribing onto the surface of a cake to give a guideline to write over, marking a shape or indicating where you will be placing a decoration or cake tier.

SILICONE OR PUSH MOULDS

Flexible moulds for making sugarpaste models, e.g. little flowers. They come in hundreds of designs.

SNAGGING

When you get a rough finish on icing pearls or trails, or a dent in the surface. You can correct snags by patting down rough peaks with a damp paint-brush, or filling holes and dents with royal icing.

SNAIL TRAIL

When icing is piped round a cake in a continuous line, using any kind of nozzle to create a textured or shaped trailing line to finish or decorate.

SOFT PEAK

A term used to describe the consistency of royal icing. When the icing is lifted from the bowl on the back of a spoon or palette knife, it will have a peak that droops down and doesn't hold a stiff shape.

SPLITTING AND FILLING

Cutting a sponge horizontally and sandwiching the sponge halves with a flavoured filling, usually buttercream.

SPOTTING

When a paste colour hasn't been mixed thoroughly into a liquid and it dries with tiny spots of colour, that intensify as they dry.

STIFF PEAK

A term used to describe the consistency of royal icing, where the icing is stiff enough to hold a very firm peak shape on the back of a spoon or palette knife.

SUGARPASTE (ROLLED FONDANT OR REGALICE)

An icing paste made from icing sugar, water and gelatin. It is usually purchased, rather than home-made, as you can buy great-quality ready-made fondant. It is used for covering cakes, boards, for making flowers, shapes and modelling cake decorations. Regalice is a brand name.

SWAG

A draping decoration made to hang around cake tiers or drape down tiers in a cascade. It's mostly made with sugarpaste, but I make a chocolate version for the Club Tropicana cake (see page 126).

TAIL

A tiny tail-like projection that forms on a piped pearl when the piping nozzle is lifted away. It spoils the roundness of pearls but can be rectified by patting down gently on the tail with a small, damp paintbrush.

TEXTURISING

A method of adding a rough pattern or detailed finish to a cake, which can be done by paletting icing, adding a piped surface or using imprint mats, pins or other tools to the iced surface.

TRIPLE DOTS (OR FILLER DOTS)

Collections of small grouped piped pearls used to decorate a cake's iced surface. A perfect way to fill space.

VEINER

A rubber, plastic or silicone mould that can be used for marking and making impressions onto petal paste or sugarpaste, to make leaves or flowers look more realistic. Now there are plunger cutters that cut out a shape and make an impression at the same time, which saves using a separate veiner.

INGREDIENTS

BUTTER: Good-quality butter, unsalted or salted to taste, always to be used at room temperature when baking or making buttercreams. It can be microwaved if needed for 10 seconds at a time until just softening.

EGGS: I use medium free-range (ideally organic) eggs in all the cake recipes, unless otherwise stated; and liquid egg white to make royal icing.

FLAVOURINGS: When using vanilla flavouring always use the best quality extract you can find, never essence. I always use Nielsen-Massey.

FLOUR: I use self-raising and plain (all-purpose) flour, I like to use Allinson for these and if using a gluten-free blend I find that Doves Farm ones always have worked well in my recipes; add a little more liquid to the recipe if you feel it's dryer, for example more egg or a couple of tablespoons of soured cream or natural yoghurt.

LIQUID PASTEURISED EGG WHITE: You can get fabulous cartons of pasteurised egg white now, which is so handy if making meringues, meringue buttercream or royal icing as this means you don't have to waste any yolk (of course you can always freeze yolks if you need to), and this is really handy and quick to use. I love the Two Chicks brand and it is widely available in supermarkets.

SUGAR: I use unrefined sugar for all my buttercreams that are caramel or chocolate based, as they are un-bleached and have a naturally rich caramel taste. I only use white icing (confectioners') sugar when making coloured cakes. I prefer Billington's unrefined cane sugar; they are my favourite.

CAKE PREPARATION

ROUND TINS

These are the measurements for one cake – most of the projects in this book are made up of two cake layers sandwiched together to make one cake tier. So for example if making a 15 cm (6 in) round cake tier, from this chart below bake two layers of 500 g (1 lb 2 oz) batter (being 1 kg/2 lb 3 oz total for the finished tier).

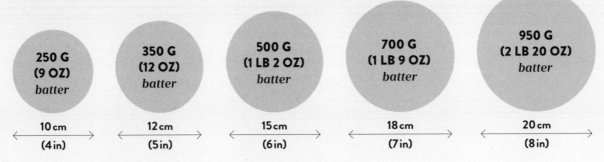

250 G (9 OZ) batter	350 G (12 OZ) batter	500 G (1 LB 2 OZ) batter	700 G (1 LB 9 OZ) batter	950 G (2 LB 20 OZ) batter
10 cm (4 in)	12 cm (5 in)	15 cm (6 in)	18 cm (7 in)	20 cm (8 in)

SQUARE TINS

Square tins need about 15 per cent more batter than round.

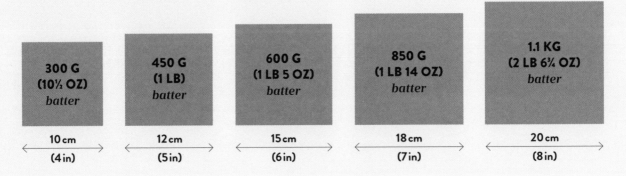

300 G (10½ OZ) batter	450 G (1 LB) batter	600 G (1 LB 5 OZ) batter	850 G (1 LB 14 OZ) batter	1.1 KG (2 LB 6¾ OZ) batter
10 cm (4 in)	12 cm (5 in)	15 cm (6 in)	18 cm (7 in)	20 cm (8 in)

I used the one-tin method in my first book, which is more foolproof when it comes to covering (as you don't have to be so skilled at filling and levelling), but with the two-cake method you get a lighter sponge. I have provided a Vanilla Bean Sponge recipe (see page 200) which you can use for a small cake, and then multiply as required. You can follow the projects in this book letter for letter, using the size of tins I've used, or change the size of the cake(s) to suit your needs. See the chart for a guide to average batter weights for each tin size, which will fill a standard cake tin just over halfway. You need to bake two separate cakes to make one cake tier. Once both cakes are baked, you can level them off and sandwich them together in place.

N O T E › *The Rich Fruit Cake (see page 210) is the only cake that's baked in just one tin.*

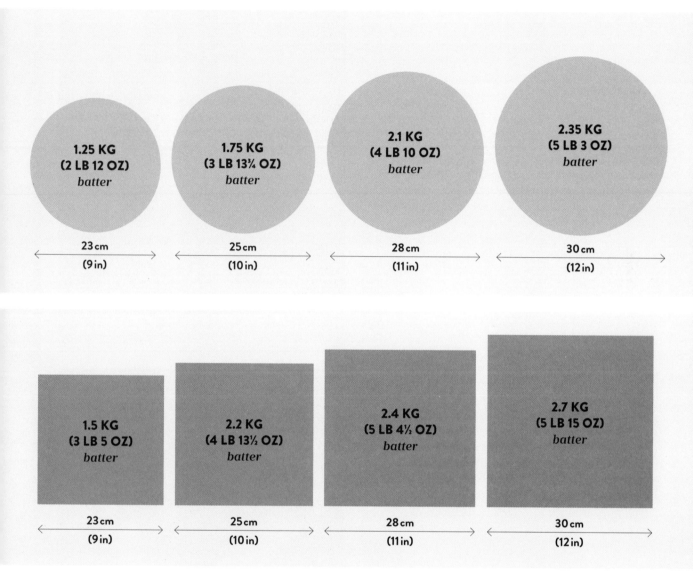

**1.25 KG
(2 LB 12 OZ)**
batter

23 cm
(9 in)

**1.75 KG
(3 LB 13¾ OZ)**
batter

25 cm
(10 in)

**2.1 KG
(4 LB 10 OZ)**
batter

28 cm
(11 in)

**2.35 KG
(5 LB 3 OZ)**
batter

30 cm
(12 in)

**1.5 KG
(3 LB 5 OZ)**
batter

23 cm
(9 in)

**2.2 KG
(4 LB 13½ OZ)**
batter

25 cm
(10 in)

**2.4 KG
(5 LB 4½ OZ)**
batter

28 cm
(11 in)

**2.7 KG
(5 LB 15 OZ)**
batter

30 cm
(12 in)

PREPARING CAKE TINS

Always line your tins. It will prevent the cakes from sticking and protect them from breaking. We line tons of tins at Fancy Nancy and my dad George (always full of clever ideas) gave me a good tip: cut a whole roll of baking parchment into strips so you've got one long strip to work with. It makes it so much quicker if you do loads of baking! Cut the roll into strips just over the tin height (line up the roll against the side of your tin so you can cut it just a bit higher than the side of the tin). This will save you cutting pieces to fit, as you can just wrap around the outside of the tin and rip off the length you need. Keep these strips pre-cut.

STUFF YOU'LL NEED

> cake tin(s)
> non-stick baking parchment
> edible-ink pen
> scissors or a small, sharp knife

> bread knife
> pastry brush
> butter, for greasing

01. Generously grease the inside of your tin with plenty of butter by smudging it all over with a piece of paper, a pastry brush or your fingers.

TIP › *Use baking parchment, not greaseproof paper. Greaseproof paper isn't substantial enough and can often disintegrate, or get baked onto the tin or cake.*

02. Wrap a strip of baking parchment around the outside of the tin, so you can rip off the whole length you need. Place the strip around the internal wall of your tin, running neatly along the base of the tin. Press it onto the butter to hold it in place.

03. Put your tin onto your rolled out baking parchment and either cut it with a sharp knife all the way round (if you have a surface you can cut onto), or draw a circle around the tin with an edible-ink pen then cut it out with scissors. Place the disc or square of parchment into the base of the tin. Now your tin is lined and your sponge will come out perfectly.

PREPARING
COOKIE TRAYS

~~~

Line the trays with baking
parchment so they don't stick
(it will damage the shape of
your cookies if you have to
pry them off the tray with
a knife). Simply cut enough
baking parchment to fit the
tray, and stick it to the tray by
dampening it with a little water,
or by dabbing the corners with
a little royal icing or cake mix.

MAKING PIPING BAGS

For cake decorating you need lots of piping bags. You can easily buy disposable ones, but it's handy (and cheaper) if you make your own, and it's pretty simple. Make 20 or so at a time: it's a good idea to keep a stock of them so you have plenty. If you have lots of colours to make for a design, you'll need a separate bag for each. I keep a running stock of 100 or so, so they're ready whenever I need them. Use baking parchment rather than greaseproof paper, as it's stronger.

45 cm (18 in)

01. Unroll the parchment and cut it at intervals of approx. 45 cm (18 in), so you end up with several large squares of parchment.

02. Cut each square diagonally across, from corner to corner, to make two triangles out of each square.

03. Lay a triangle on the work surface in front of you with the longest straight edge away from you and the wider point facing towards you. Take one corner from the edge furthest away from you, and bring this outer corner in to meet the point facing you. Pull it in tightly so that a cone shape starts to form.

04. Hold the corners together tightly and lift up the cone in front of you.

Bring the other corner in by wrapping it around behind your cone, to meet your thumb that's holding the first part together. Swiftly slip the new corner under your thumb carefully, not letting go of the other corner.

05. Check there's a sharp point at the end of the bag. If it's not sharp you can play with it by pulling the cone tighter with your thumbs and fingers. If you don't get it right the first time, keep trying; it takes a few goes for you to get the feel of it.

06. To fix the piping bag, tear into the join in a couple of places and fold the bag in to secure, or use a stapler (but take care that no stray staples find their way into your icing).

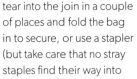

wrap the free corner around and behind the cone

02

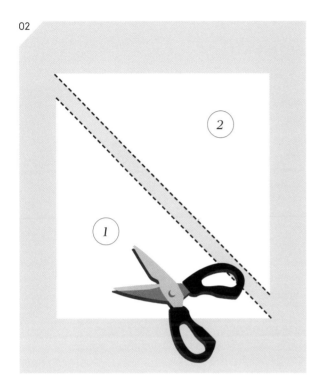

①

②

03

widest edge away from you
↓

05

check the point is sharp

06

secure by folding or stapling

SPLITTING, FILLING & COVERING CAKES

FILLING & CRUMB-COATING WITH BUTTERCREAM

Your lovely sponge cake needs a delicious filling to add flavour and stick it together. I also recommend giving the filled sponge a 'crumb coat', coating it with buttercream before covering with marzipan, more buttercream, icing or sugarpaste: this seals in the sponge and covers any lumps and bumps, giving you a smooth base coat. It's also called 'dirty icing' in the States (not the most pleasant of terms, really!).

STUFF YOU'LL NEED

Equipment:
› cake leveller
› cake drum (the same size and shape as your cake)
› pastry brush
› palette knife
› small spirit level (optional)
› cake drum approx. 5 cm (2 in) larger than your cake
› side scraper (optional)
› straight edge tool (or plastic 30 cm/12 in ruler)
› small, sharp knife
› turntable

Ingredients:
› 2 same-sized sponge cakes
› Vanilla Soaking Syrup (see page 202, optional)
› buttercream
› curd or jam

01

TIP › *If you are making a multi-tiered cake you need to make sure every cake stands at the same height before you cover them, so that your tiers look even. For example, if you are making a round cake with 15 cm (6 in) , 20 cm (8 in) and 25 cm (10 in) tiers, take all 6 cakes (you need 2 cakes per tier) and lay them out on a work surface. Pick the lowest one (all cakes rise differently during the baking process and vary a little). Trim each cake down by cutting off the domed top with a cake leveller or bread knife, to match the height of the lowest cake, so you end up with 6 cakes all standing at the same height.*

04

01. Start by trimming off the domed tops of your sponges, so that you're left with two sponges with flat tops (see pic 01). This will enable you to neatly sandwich them together. →

~~~

Place another cake board on the top of the sandwiched cake and push the sponge together, checking that it is completely level and to push out any excess filling. If you want to be really exact, sit a little spirit level on top of the board. If the cake is slightly higher on one side, push down where you need to until it has levelled out.

07

02. Take one sponge and place it crust-side down on the cake drum of the same size, securing it with a little buttercream spread onto the drum (see pic 02 on previous page). Sometimes you'll find your sponge may have shrunk a tiny bit so it seems a tad smaller than the drum, so just make sure it's centred (see pic 03 on previous page).

~~~

03. Brush the cut side of the sponge with a little sugar syrup, if you like. Spread an even layer of buttercream over the top of the base sponge half with a palette knife (see pic 04 on previous page); if you use too much, you'll find the buttercream oozes out of the middle when you cover it with marzipan or icing and you end up with a bulge. Spread a little jam over the other cake sponge (see pic 05 on previous page). If you want to add more filling, split your sponges in half to add further layers. The more you split the sponge, the more likely you have to patch it up before covering to make it look neat.

TIP › *If you do split your sponges further, it's worth following a tip my dad, George, came up with: before slicing the cake in half, score a line all the way down one edge of the cake with a serrated knife, so that you can line the halves back up again when you sandwich the sponge back together.*

~~~

04. Take the top half of sponge and place it over the bottom half to sandwich the two halves together and line up the cakes (see pic 06 on previous page).

~~~

05. Transfer the filled cake to the larger cake drum and place it on the turntable. Now, crumb coat. Using a palette knife, generously spread a thin layer of buttercream all over the sponge, making sure the surface is completely covered (see pic 07). This will help to fill in the middle layer, where there is a ridge, and smooth out any excess filling, and will also mask any

08

small holes in your sponge. If you have a side scraper, sweep it around the side of the cake in a continuous motion, holding it at a 90-degree angle to the cake board and using the cake drum at the base as a guide. Spin the turntable around as you pull the scraper towards you, leaving you with a smooth, thin coat. If your cake is square, scrape it on each side, sharpening off the coating at the corners. Once all the sides are neat, use the straight edge tool or ruler, held at a 45-degree angle to the surface, dragging it across the top of the sponge towards you, in one continuous motion, to smooth the cake's surface and take off any excess buttercream (see pic 08). Once you are happy with your crumb-coated sponge, pop into the fridge for a couple of hours, or the freezer for 30 minutes, so it firms up and holds its shape when you cover it with your first layer of rolled-out icing or marzipan.

Your cake is now ready to ice and decorate. You can pipe all manner of decorations directly onto a crumb-coated sponge, or cover it with marzipan, chocolate or sugarpaste.

PREPARING RICH FRUIT CAKE BEFORE COVERING

~~~

Invert the baked cake over the cake board to reveal the flat bottom of the fruit cake, which will be smoother and more level than the top of the cake.

Stick the fruit cake to the correct-sized cake board by brushing the board with a little boiled jam and sticking on a few small pieces of marzipan.

You need to get the sides and top of the cake as straight and square as possible to get the best finish, so if your cake is not quite level or has holes in the edges, smooth them out before your start by plugging them with marzipan. This means that when you cover the cake with marzipan or icing, you won't get any lumps or bumps.

The fruit cake may shrink a bit, leaving a gap at the base of the cake when you invert the sponge onto the board. If you have got a gap, fill it with a sausage of marzipan or sugarpaste, all around the base, so that when you cover the cake it will sit flush straight down to the base board. If the cake is not level, trim down the higher side to level it out, or add a little marzipan to build up the lower part before covering it with marzipan. Taking care at the first stage, before covering the cake, will leave you with a more professional finish.

COVERING CAKES WITH MARZIPAN & SUGARPASTE (OR CHOCOLATE PASTE)

I've used a few different coverings for the cake projects in this book. Some are coated in buttercream and some are coated in ganache, but most are covered with a layer of marzipan and sugarpaste or chocolate paste. Marzipan has a high oil content so preserves the sponge for a little longer, and it sets nice and firmly.

A round or sculpted cake, or a soft-edged square cake, is generally covered in one large piece of rolled-out marzipan, that is laid over the top of the cake and draped around each side in one piece.

However, some designs, e.g. sharp-edged royal-iced cakes, require boxed edges, so a round cake would need a piece of marzipan laid on the top, then the sides covered with one long strip, cut against the top with a sharp knife to create a boxy sharp edge, rather than a rounded corner.

For square cakes, each side is 'panelled' with a piece of marzipan and cut sharply at each edge with a knife. For my Vintage Floral Patchwork Cake (see page 139), I use a panelled square sponge for each tier, rather than the conventional method below. For covering moulded cakes, see the Old-school Trainer project on page 57.

~~~~~~~~

The chart below gives a guide to the amounts of marzipan and sugarpaste you need to cover different-sized cakes. All my cakes end up about 10 cm (4 in) deep once iced (including the

ROUND CAKES: *Marzipan or sugarpaste needed*

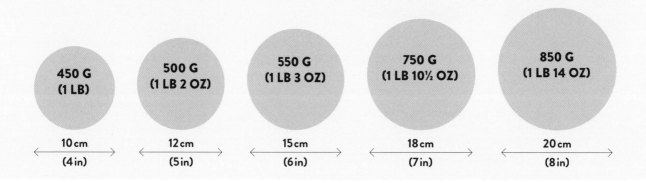

450 G (1 LB)	500 G (1 LB 2 OZ)	550 G (1 LB 3 OZ)	750 G (1 LB 10½ OZ)	850 G (1 LB 14 OZ)
10 cm (4 in)	12 cm (5 in)	15 cm (6 in)	18 cm (7 in)	20 cm (8 in)

SQUARE CAKES: *Marzipan or sugarpaste needed*

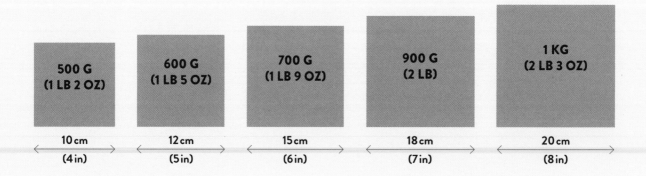

500 G (1 LB 2 OZ)	600 G (1 LB 5 OZ)	700 G (1 LB 9 OZ)	900 G (2 LB)	1 KG (2 LB 3 OZ)
10 cm (4 in)	12 cm (5 in)	15 cm (6 in)	18 cm (7 in)	20 cm (8 in)

cake drum and two layers of sponge, sandwiched together with buttercream). If you are covering a deeper or shallower cake, tweak these quantities accordingly.

If you have an irregular shaped cake, e.g. a heart or a hexagon, roll out the quantity I've suggested for a square cake, to be on the safe side. I always roll out more than I need, to make sure I don't have to mess about stretching or filling gaps. Any excess can be re-used. Cut off the excess as soon as you've laid it over the cake, before it gets too crumbly.

TIP › *If you want to make a huge square cake you can stick four smaller square sponges together to make one large slab of sponge. E.g. for a 40 cm (16 in) square cake, place*

4 x 20 cm/8 in squares on a 40 cm (16 in) drum, join them together with buttercream and fill to make one huge cake.

TIP › *If you are working on a standard height cake tier it will be approximately 9–10 cm (3.5–4 in) depth. So you will need to roll out a large circle of at least 45 cm (18 in) diameter, to allow for twice the depth of the cake plus the diameter across the top. I always recommend to measure the sides of the cake once split and filled and crumb coated then you can be sure your rolled out covering will fit over the top as well as reaching the base without any gaps.*

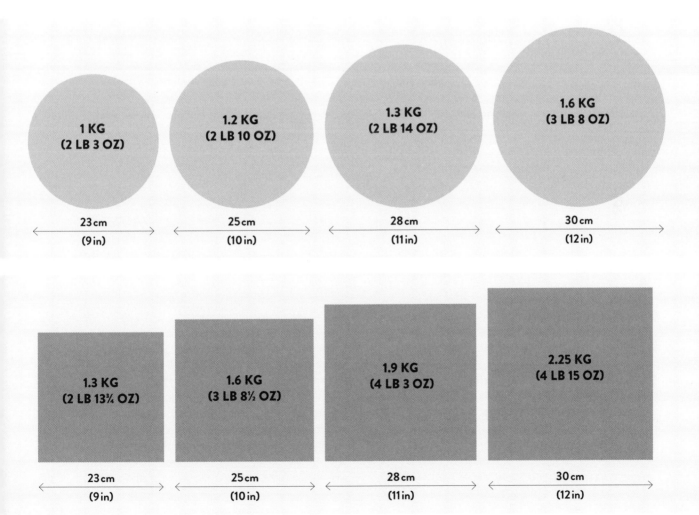

1 KG (2 LB 3 OZ)	**1.2 KG** (2 LB 10 OZ)	**1.3 KG** (2 LB 14 OZ)	**1.6 KG** (3 LB 8 OZ)
23 cm (9 in)	25 cm (10 in)	28 cm (11 in)	30 cm (12 in)
1.3 KG (2 LB 13¾ OZ)	**1.6 KG** (3 LB 8½ OZ)	**1.9 KG** (4 LB 3 OZ)	**2.25 KG** (4 LB 15 OZ)
23 cm (9 in)	25 cm (10 in)	28 cm (11 in)	30 cm (12 in)

THE FIRST COAT: *Covering with Marzipan*

Apply marzipan (see chart on page 172–73 for quantities) to your cake in the same way you cover it with sugarpaste (see steps below), but rather than coating the surface with vodka or boiled water, use jam. You need the surface of the cake to be sticky so that the marzipan will adhere to it; I find apricot jam works well. Once the cake is iced with both coats, leave it to dry for a day before decorating. Avoid cakey stress by planning your cake project well ahead of time so that you don't need to rush.

THE SECOND COAT: *Covering with sugarpaste*

STUFF YOU'LL NEED

Equipment
> pastry brush
> plastic rolling pin
> guide sticks or marzipan spacers (optional) (see page 224 for stockists)
> top smoother
> 2 side smoothers
> turntable
> spare cake drum, 5–7.5 cm (2–3 in), larger than the cake
> small, sharp knife
> pin tool or pin

Ingredients
> a little vodka (or cool boiled water)
> a cake, split and filled, covered in marzipan and stuck to a cake board with buttercream
> icing (confectioners') sugar, for dusting
> sugarpaste (see pages 172–73 for quantities)

TIP › *If you don't like marzipan, or have a nut allergy, use sugarpaste instead of marzipan for the first coat.*

01. Place the cake on a clean surface then, with a pastry brush, cover the surface of the cake with the vodka (see pic 01).

02. Dust the work surface with a little icing sugar, and knead the sugarpaste until it feels soft and malleable (see pic 02). Start rolling out the sugarpaste, rolling it from the middle outwards, turning it as you go and trying to retain a round shape. Sweep plenty of icing sugar under the sugarpaste so it doesn't stick to the surface, and dust the top of the sugarpaste with icing sugar, too. Don't flip the sugarpaste over as this will make it too dry and more likely to crack once it's on the cake.

Try to roll the sugarpaste to the same even thickness, so that it's not too thin (it could rip), and avoid bumps in the sugarpaste, too. If you want to make your life easier, invest in a pair of guide sticks or sugarpaste spacers, which will guarantee an even thickness, giving you a smooth, level

surface on the cake (see pic 03). Use a top smoother to polish the sugarpaste and smooth out any ridges that may have been left by the rolling pin.

TIP › *If the room you're working in is really chilly, or your sugarpaste feels too hard, give it a 10-second blast in the microwave until it's a little warmer and easier to work with.*

03. Sprinkle the rolled-out sugarpaste with a little icing sugar and roll it gently over the rolling pin by placing the pin at the back and rolling it towards your body so that you have the sugarpaste wrapped around the pin. This allows you to line it up in the centre of the cake so you can check you've got enough to cover all of the sides. Hold the rolling pin above the cake, with the centre of the pin lining up roughly in the middle of the cake (see pic 04). Before unrolling onto the cake, make sure you have enough sugarpaste draping over the side in front of you, then quickly roll out the covering away from you over the top of the cake. The excess should drape around the sides of the cake. Rolling the sugarpaste onto the cake like this, rather than draping it over your arms, helps prevent air bubbles becoming trapped under it. →

04. As quickly as you can, smooth the sugarpaste onto the cake, using your hands to smooth the top, working from the centre outwards towards the edges, making sure to press out any air that may be trapped under the marzipan. Use a top smoother to polish the top and sides, gently pressing and smoothing over the surface.

05. Once the top is smooth, gently press around the top edge to drape the sugarpaste down over the sides, being careful not to pull it down or it may rip. Smooth the sugarpaste around the sides, taking care not to create any folds or creases (see pic 05). If it looks like the sugarpaste might crease or bunch up, gently lift the sugarpaste up again just where the crease is beginning to show, then push the fold towards the base of the cake drum.

06. When your cake is covered with sugarpaste, take a small knife and cut away as much excess as you can (see pic 06), leaving just a small border of sugarpaste lying on the work surface (approx. 2.5 cm/1 in). Save the trimmings if you like, but put them in a bag and seal the bag immediately, as sugarpaste dries out quickly.

07. For a professional finish, lift the cake up from the table and hold it underneath in the centre of the cake drum so that you can see the little excess 'skirt' of sugarpaste hanging down a little way below the bottom of the cake drum. With a cake smoother, gently press the sugarpaste onto the sides of the cake right to the edge of the cake drum (see pic 07). Press all the way around the cake until you are content that it is smooth and even.

NOTE › *Some people have difficulty lifting cakes, particularly if they are quite large. If you have a turntable, use a few cake boards smaller than the cake to elevate it and allow you to smooth the sugarpaste down, or if you don't have one, find something in your kitchen that you can use in its place to raise the cake – an upturned bowl perhaps, or a few smaller cake boards stacked on top of a tea towel.*

08. Take a small, sharp, clean knife and, holding it at a 90-degree angle to the side of the cake, run it all the way along the underside of the cake board, trimming off the excess sugarpaste and letting it to drop onto the work surface, leaving you with a neatly cut bottom edge (see pic 08).

08

09

09. Place the perfectly trimmed cake onto a spare cake drum and transfer the cake and drum to your turntable. Use all three smoothers to gently smooth over the whole cake, spinning it around and working as quickly as you can (see pic 09).

~~~~~~~~~~

10. Now you can pay more attention to the cake's surface and sides. Check for air bubbles under the surface, and if you find any gently insert a pin tool or pin into them to expel the air by gently pressing it out through the hole, then smooth the hole with your fingers. Bend down so you have the cake at eye level, then judge the straightness of the top and sides. Smooth over the top, sides and edges again with side smoothers, using a firm pressure, until you are pleased with the finish.

~~~~~~~~~~

11. Leave the covered cake to dry overnight. Check again for any air bubbles. Sometimes, inevitably, you will miss some bubbles and come back the next day to see a huge bulge under the icing or coating. Though this is frustrating, all you can do is pop them with the pin tool and gently smooth over with a side or top smoother. If your cake is going to be covered in decorations it shouldn't matter too much, but if it's going to be a simple chic cake with a lot of exposed icing surface, there may be some cracking now, as the surface would have dried out a bit. Don't worry too much – this can be disguised with royal icing. You are always going to get the odd lump and bump and it really shouldn't matter too much if you are going to be adding additional decoration to the cake's surface once it's iced.

COLOURING SUGARPASTE OR FONDANT

~~~

Sugarpaste, fondant, marzipan, petal paste and modelling paste can all be coloured before they are applied to a cake. I favour paste colours, as they are very concentrated and you only need a little. Gel colours aren't quite as strong, so you'll need more. Avoid using liquid colours for pliable coverings, as it can change the consistency of the covering and make it too sticky. If you are unsure of a colour's intensity, or have a colour you haven't used before, test it on a spare piece of sugarpaste first.

Knead the paste on the work surface until it is soft and pliable. You may need to add a little icing (confectioners') sugar to prevent it sticking, but don't use too much as it will dry it out. Roll it into a sausage shape then, using a toothpick, take a little of your chosen colour out of its pot. Spread the colour across the sausage, bearing in mind that it's easier to add more than it is to remove it or dilute it. Fold the ends of the sausage inwards onto the centre of the sausage, to cover the colour and push it down. Knead the colour into the paste, then roll the paste flat a few times, folding it before rolling again, to evenly distribute the colour. If you are making a large quantity of coloured paste, break off a small piece of paste mid-knead, before the colour is fully incorporated, and knead it until the colour is even and no marbling remains (leaving the rest of the paste in a food bag). This will give you a good indication of the final shade, and you can see if you need to add more colour (or more white) before kneading the whole piece. If you are kneading colour into a large amount of paste, break off small pieces and knead them separately while leaving the other bits in a food bag, to avoid it drying out, then combine all the pieces at the end in one final mix.

CAKE BUILDING

STACKING TIERED CAKES WITH DOWELS

If you want to make a tiered cake creation, there are several different ways that you can present it. My favourite way is with hidden plastic cake dowels, so that the tiers are stacked directly on top of each other, creating a one-piece cake design.

There are many ways to create multi-tiered cakes, including using special tiered stands, polystyrene plinths or special pillars, but in this book most of the stacked cake designs are in one piece, with the exception of the Vintage Floral Patchwork Cake (see page 139).

If you follow these steps, stacking with dowels is relatively simple. Planning in advance is key. Before you decide on your cake design, ask yourself a few questions:

Does the cake need to be stacked before decorating?
If you are making a cake with sugar decorations or flowing patterns going across the cake tiers, it's easier to stack the tiers first.

Do you need to transport the cake?
If the design allows, you could keep all the tiers separate; dowel each one but do not stick them together, decorate them all, then just stack and finish them on site. All you need to do is take along some royal icing and a palette knife to lift the cakes onto each other when you are there; as long as you have dowelled it at home and checked it's level it will be fairly stress free.

Are you going to be able to transport your stacked cake?
If your cake is more than two tiers, some models of car won't have space for them in the boot. Cakes must be placed in the boot on a flat base. Do not place a stacked cake on a seat or, even worse, on someone's lap! If you need to travel 300 miles in a car through rural country lanes, it's probably best not to drive with a fully constructed five-tier cake. Think about the weight of a finished stacked cake, too. They are very heavy when decorated: a five-tier cake can weigh about 30 kg (66 lb)!

Don't worry; if you plan in advance, and decide to build a large pre-stacked cake, as long as you have dowelled your cake correctly and follow the steps opposite and over the page, you will be fine.

~~~~~~~~

TIP › *Always take a repair kit with you if you are setting up a tiered cake at a venue. If you find hairline cracks or larger cracks on the lower tiers, it means you haven't used enough dowels. Don't worry, if the cracks are small you can fill them with a little royal icing and they will magically disappear.*

STUFF YOU'LL NEED ›

Equipment
› cake dummies or drums (the same size as your cakes)
› pin or scriber tool
› cake dowels (preferably heavy-duty white plastic – see page 224 for stockists)

› edible-ink pen
› spare ridged wood decking (optional – see TIP on page 181)
› small hacksaw
› stiff royal icing
› palette knife

Ingredients
› iced cakes

01. Use a cake dummy or drum as a guide to mark out a circle or square the same size as the cake board from the cake that will be sitting on top of the bottom tier (see pic 01). For example, if you are stacking an 18 cm (7 in) round cake on top of a 25 cm (10 in) round base cake, place an 18 cm (7 in) round cake dummy or drum on the base cake as a guide, marking around it with a scriber tool, pin, or the tip of a sharp knife. The scored line will show you where you need to place the dowels (within the line). If you have more than two tiers, repeat on the other tiers, except the top tier.

~~~~~~~~

02. By eye, push the cake dowels into the base cake, until they touch the cake board at the bottom of the cake, taking care to put them in straight, not leaning at an angle (see pic 02). Place the dowels all around the inside edge of the scored outline, then pop a few in the middle just to be safe. I recommend being over-cautious and using plenty of dowels, particularly in the base tier if there will be more than one tier above it. If in doubt, use loads! If you just have a teensy top-tier cake, you don't need to put many dowels in – four regular dowels will be plenty for a 10 cm (4 in) cake. →

~~~~~~~~

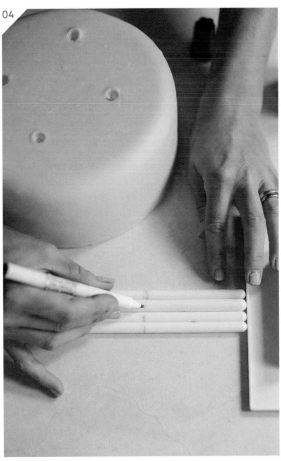

03. Once all the dowels are inserted into your cake, use an edible-ink pen to mark the dowels, level with the iced surface of the cake (see pic 03). Mark them all, even though your surface is pretty straight, as there will be slight undulations, and you will see that when you remove the dowels and line them up together against a flat edge to trim them down. Remove all the dowels.

~~~~~~~~~

04. To ensure your next cake will be level, re-mark all of the dowels to be the same length as the tallest depth mark (see pic 04). This way, you won't get the cake above pressing on the cake below. Don't worry if there is the odd gap in between the tiers – they can be filled with royal icing or disguised with ribbon or pearl piping (see Wedgwood-Inspired White-on-White Wedding Cake on page 72), which is far preferable to your cake cracking under the weight of the cake on top. Cut the dowels down to the marks with a small hacksaw, brushing off any of the plastic from the hacksaw, then place them back into your cake, ready to receive the tier above (see pic 05).

~~~~~~~~~

TIP › *My dad George had a genius idea for cutting dowels safely, as he is a bit (a lot) of a worrier. He got an off-cut of ridged decking from a timber yard, which the dowels sit in snugly, so when you are cutting through them they don't slip around on the surface risking a serious injury! It does make life easier. We keep a piece in the drawer with the hacksaw and dowels.*

05. Once all your cakes have dowels inserted, they are ready to stack. Spread a little stiff royal icing on the middle of the cake underneath, then line up the cake above, and position it carefully on top (see pic 06). If it's a small cake, you can do this with your hands without damaging the icing, but if it's a large cake, use a heavy-duty palette knife to lift it on and line it up before placing onto the cake below.

ICING CAKE DRUMS

Many of the designs in this book are finished and displayed on a cake drum iced with sugarpaste, to give them a professional touch and complete the design. I think it looks really messy and unfinished if you place a beautiful cake onto an un-iced drum.

Icing a cake drum is easy, and can be done in advance (at least 24 hours in advance is ideal, so the icing has time to dry and doesn't get squeezed over the edge by the weight of the cake). Sugarpaste has a very long shelf-life!

Cakes are usually placed on a board 5–8 cm (2–3 in) larger than the cake, unless your design involves lots of decoration or models on the board, in which case you might want a larger board.

Consider the colour you want to ice the board in: you might want to use the same colour icing that you use to decorate your cake, or perhaps choose a contrasting colour.

As well as iced cake boards for one large cake, you can also make a multi-tiered cake display stand for mini cakes or cupcakes, by making a tower of different sized drums, e.g. a four-tier tower with 20 cm (8 in), 25 cm (10 in), 30 cm (12 in) and 35 cm (14 in) pre-iced boards, with each level elevated using polystyrene cake dummies or separators as a central column (see page 224 for stockists), covered in ribbon, several inches smaller than the boards (to allow room for the cakes).

This chart is a guide for the approximate weight of sugarpaste you need for different sized drums.

ROUND DRUMS: *Sugarpaste needed*

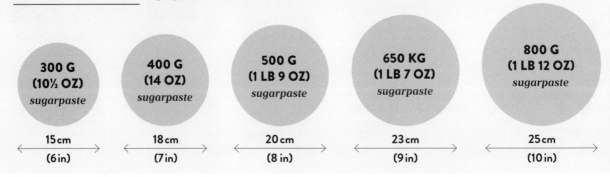

300 G (10½ OZ) sugarpaste	400 G (14 OZ) sugarpaste	500 G (1 LB 9 OZ) sugarpaste	650 KG (1 LB 7 OZ) sugarpaste	800 G (1 LB 12 OZ) sugarpaste
15 cm (6 in)	18 cm (7 in)	20 cm (8 in)	23 cm (9 in)	25 cm (10 in)

SQUARE DRUMS: *Sugarpaste needed*

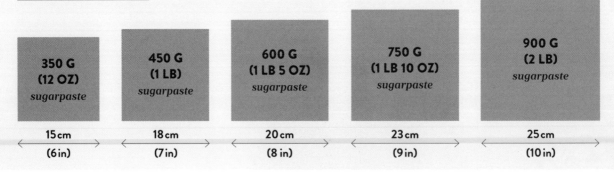

350 G (12 OZ) sugarpaste	450 G (1 LB) sugarpaste	600 G (1 LB 5 OZ) sugarpaste	750 G (1 LB 10 OZ) sugarpaste	900 G (2 LB) sugarpaste
15 cm (6 in)	18 cm (7 in)	20 cm (8 in)	23 cm (9 in)	25 cm (10 in)

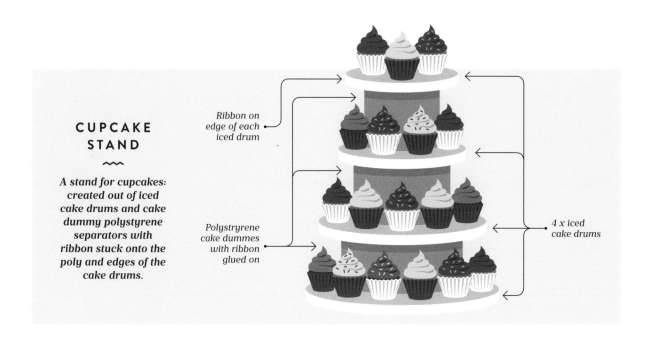

CUPCAKE STAND

~~~

A stand for cupcakes: created out of iced cake drums and cake dummy polystyrene separators with ribbon stuck onto the poly and edges of the cake drums.

Ribbon on edge of each iced drum

Polystryrene cake dummes with ribbon glued on

4 x iced cake drums

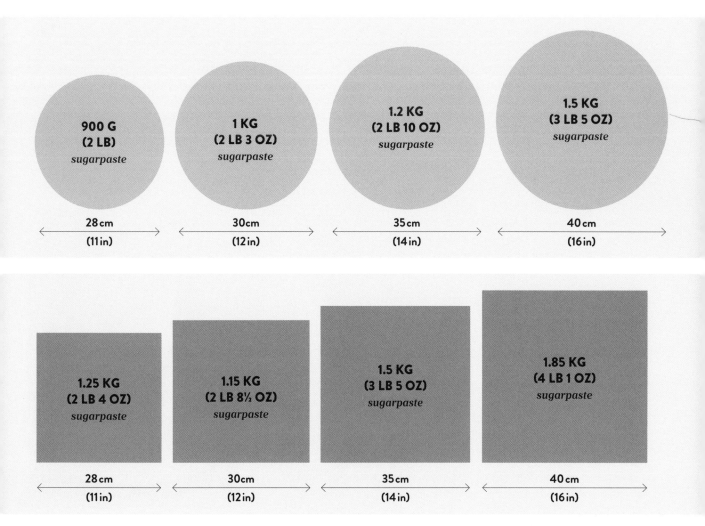

900 G
(2 LB)
sugarpaste

28 cm
(11 in)

1 KG
(2 LB 3 OZ)
sugarpaste

30cm
(12 in)

1.2 KG
(2 LB 10 OZ)
sugarpaste

35 cm
(14 in)

1.5 KG
(3 LB 5 OZ)
sugarpaste

40 cm
(16 in)

1.25 KG
(2 LB 4 OZ)
sugarpaste

28 cm
(11 in)

1.15 KG
(2 LB 8½ OZ)
sugarpaste

30cm
(12 in)

1.5 KG
(3 LB 5 OZ)
sugarpaste

35 cm
(14 in)

1.85 KG
(4 LB 1 OZ)
sugarpaste

40 cm
(16 in)

STUFF YOU'LL NEED

- › icing (confectioners') sugar, for dusting
- › cake drum
- › pastry brush
- › vodka or cooled boiled water
- › sugarpaste, to cover
- › large plastic rolling pin
- › guide sticks
- › pin or scriber tool
- › top smoother
- › sharp knife

01. Dust the cake board with a little icing sugar, then use a pastry brush to wet it with vodka or cooled boiled water (see pic 01). This will help stick the rolled-out icing to the board, preventing it from sliding around when you are trimming off the edges.

02. Knead the sugarpaste until pliable, then dust plenty of icing sugar over the work surface beneath the icing (see pic 02). Flatten out the sugarpaste and roll it out evenly from the middle outwards, turning the sugarpaste regularly to prevent it getting misshapen; you want a nice square piece to lay over the cake drum (see pic 03). Use guide sticks if you have them, or, if not, take care to roll with even pressure so that the sugarpaste has an even thickness of 5–6 mm (approx. ½ in).

TIP › *If you get too much icing sugar on the surface of a dark-coloured icing, especially black, the icing sugar will mark it with white blotches that are very hard to remove – if in doubt, strip it off, re-knead and do it again.*

03. Lift up the board and hold it just above the rolled out icing to check it's big enough, then place it back on the work surface (see pic 04). Lift the rolled sugarpaste carefully over both arms or roll onto

your rolling pin to lift, and place it on your dampened cake board (see pic 05). If you have too little icing or it's not in a square shape, strip it off and re-roll it. Make sure there are no air bubbles under the icing. You should be able to see them if you bend down and check the board at eye level. If you can see any, use a pin or scriber tool to pierce a small hole in the icing and push out the air gently with your fingertips.

04. Smooth over the iced board with the top smoother (see pic 06), to rub out any lumps and bumps and give it a polished finish.

05. Hold the cake board up with one hand. Take a sharp knife and carefully cut all the way around the edge to remove the excess icing. Hold the knife at a 90-degree angle and use the edge of the board as a guide (see pic 07). Turn the cake board as you go, and let the icing fall onto the surface beneath (you can re-use this). Alternatively, place the board on a turntable and hold the knife in place while you rotate the board.

06. Make sure the edge is neat by gently smoothing round the edge of the board with your fingertips. Leave the board to dry for at least 24 hours, until you need it.

DECORATING WITH ROYAL ICING

Royal icing is essential for cake decorating. You can use it for so many things: fixing mistakes, sticking cakes together, adding ribbons, decorating cookies, or sticking decorations on. I use it throughout this book. It's like a sugary cement, as it sets rock hard. Make your recipe to the 'stiff peak' consistency (see below), then you can water it down to the other two consistencies, for a multitude of uses. Royal icing lasts for about a week in a container or food bag, and you can freeze it. It's also very easy to colour; paste colours are ideal (rather than liquid colours) because you don't need to use so much that it loosens the consistency. You can buy ready-made royal icing in supermarkets if you only need a little, perhaps for basic piping or a message. I used it when I first started out, back in the old days!
Makes enough royal icing to cover and decorate a three-tier cake

STUFF YOU'LL NEED

› 250 g (9 oz/2 cups) sifted icing (confectioners') sugar
› 1 medium egg white (30 g/1 oz)

› juice of ½ lemon (approx. 2 tablespoons)

TIP › *Roll your lemon firmly on the work surface before cutting and juicing, and it will yield more juice. Don't ask me how, it just does. It's magic. My lovely friend Alison Penn who is a food genius (and fabulous loyal staff member for many, many years) taught me this trick.*

Place all the ingredients in a large bowl or in the bowl of a stand mixer fitted with the paddle attachment. Whisk by hand or on the slow speed for about 5 minutes, until all the powdery sugar has disappeared and the mixture is very stiff. If you need a little more liquid, add a dash more lemon juice; if the mixture's too wet, add a little more sugar. You want to achieve a thick paste consistency that isn't powdery dry and holds its shape. Beat slowly for about 3 minutes to eliminate lumps and make a smooth icing.

In the world of cake decorating, you need to get the right consistency of royal icing for each job, and we call these 'stiff peak', 'soft peak' and 'runny'.

STIFF PEAK

This icing should be stiff and paste-like, so that when you lift up a spoon from the mixture you get a stiff 'peak', or peaks, forming. This means that whatever you pipe will hold its shape. Stiff peak is used for 'snail trails', beads and other piped shapes, and is used to stick decorations onto cakes, stick cakes to their iced drums or stick cake tiers together. You may need a few drops of water so the icing pushes out of the nozzle (you don't want to squeeze so hard that it hurts your hand), but you want it to hold its shape. It should look very spiky and rigid, and so stiff it almost looks dry. It sets very hard, so can hold the weight of a large decoration.

SOFT PEAK

This is stiff-peak icing 'let down' or loosened with a few drops of water, or egg white (pasteurised) if you prefer, so that it flows freely from your icing bag. It's not completely runny – a line will still hold its shape – but if you were to pipe a pearl trim with it, the pearls would sink into a wavy blobby line. Soft-peak is used for piping messages onto cakes and outlining shapes of cookies or run-outs. To test that the consistency is right, just add a few drops of water at a time until the icing feels easier to stir and is looser. Don't make it too runny! It should still hold a peak but the peak should just flop slightly.

TIP › *Rather than adding water directly to the icing, run a spoon under a tap with a little icing on and stir this into the icing to prevent making it too runny. You only need a small amount of liquid to loosen the consistency.* →

RUNNY

This consistency is used for 'flooding' outlines on run-outs or cookies, to create coloured sections. Ideally the surface of runny icing settles flat and smooths over at about the 10-second mark. You don't want it to run out of the piping bag too quickly. If you find the icing doesn't quite settle flat, either shake the cookie gently or, if you are making run-outs on a film or acetate sheet, pop this onto a cake board (tape the edges down) and gently bang the board on the work surface to encourage the icing to sit neat and flat.

If you want to colour runny icing, colour it at the stiff-peak stage, then let it down after you have coloured it. This way you won't thin out your perfect runny consistency after you've got it just right.

RUNNY

TOP TIP

To test if the consistency is right, take a palette knife or spoon and drag it through the bowl of icing about a few centimetres (couple of inches) deep. Count how many seconds pass until the line you made disappears and the icing has returned to a flat surface. If the surface of the icing smooths over in about 10 seconds then your icing is ready to use. If it takes longer, then the icing is too thick, so slowly add a few more drops of water. If your icing surface smooths over in less than 5–10 seconds, it is too runny. Slowly add more sifted icing sugar to thicken it or add a little more stiff-peak icing.

STIFF PEAK

SOFT PEAK

PIPING OVER SNAGS, HOLES & FILLING GAPS

Royal icing is a fabulous edible Polyfilla! If you have had to prick a hole in an air bubble, leave a gap, or pick a bit of decoration off, you may be left with a hole or a mark. Most designs allow for you to go over these with another decoration, but if not, and you are piping stripes or having a clean iced surface, or laying your ribbon over and you have a bumpy hole, you can just pipe over it with stiff royal icing to fill. If you've made holes with a pin or cocktail stick and they are quite visible, pipe a little royal icing into the hole and wipe off the excess with a clean dry finger and nobody will ever know it was there.

MAKING RUN-OUTS WITH ROYAL ICING

Making run-outs involves making a shape by piping a frame or outline in a line, e.g. around the edge of a cookie, then filling it in, or 'flooding' it with a slightly more liquid 'runny' icing to fill in the shape, creating a coloured pattern or picture. I use the technique for my Celebrookies and the cute Christmas Kitsch Cookies (see pages 69 and 122). The technique is fairly straightforward and can be used directly on cookies and cakes, or on a piece of plastic film (see page 224 for stockists) or wax paper to make a decoration that can be dried and then placed on a cake.

For small details, run-outs or large cake toppers, it helps to 'trace' over a picture, especially if you are not a naturally gifted artist. Just print out a picture then place acetate paper, cellophane, clear film wrap or wax paper over the picture and use it to trace over and copy the shape and colours.

TIP › *If you are not piping directly onto a cake or cookie it works well to pipe onto document wallets that you get from the stationers. That way you can have your image inside the wallet that you want to 'trace over' and it keeps the paper still, too.*

TIP › *Rubbing a small amount of vegetable fat or a tiny bit of sunflower oil onto the sheet or document wallet will help the icing release easily without sticking once it's dry. Just rub a tiny amount between your fingertips and smooth over.*

CREATING MARBLED, SWIRLED OR FEATHERED DESIGNS

Sometimes called 'feathering' or 'swirling', marbling is a great way to create a colourful effect with royal icing, when more than one colour is used in a base coat of icing and a cocktail stick or skewer is dragged through the colours to give a marbled or swirly effect. See the Christmas Kitsch Cookies on page 122 for an example of how to create this marbling effect with royal icing.

PIPING TECHNIQUES

Piping onto a cake is a great decoration technique. It might be simply piping a name or an inscription, or you might fancy adding texture to the surface of your cake with piped designs, either free-flowing or regimented patterns. If you are good at hand writing or drawing, free-hand piping designs might come easier to you. If you're not great at free-hand drawing or writing, you can still decorate cakes with piping but you may find it easier to go over a template or marked design and follow that. Here are some simple ways to decorate your cakes using piping.

PERSONALISING CAKES OR BOARDS WITH PIPED MESSAGES

To write a message onto a cake or a cake board, pipe on the lettering with royal icing. I like to use a No. 2 nozzle (No. 3 is too chunky and No. 1.5 can be too fine, unless your cake is tiny). Write your message on the cake as you would write with a pen. Everyone has different handwriting, so if you are a messy writer you may prefer to print out a message from the computer and mark it out onto the dry cake icing: place the printed message over the iced surface and prick out dots along the lines with a pin. Follow these dots to make a neater inscription. It's preferable to have the message sitting at the front of the cake.

TIP › *I like to score a straight line on the cake with a pin tool, which I can follow to write my message and ensure I don't go off in a wonky line. Or you can pipe the message on the surface just in front of your iced cake board, so you can see where to place the letters and how much space a message will fill. If you are nervous or new to piping, write your message in white royal icing first, then if you make a mistake you can just wipe it away with a sharp knife and start again without having stained the iced cake or board. After an hour or so, once the white icing message has set, trace over the icing with your chosen colour. The letters will stand out more, as they are lifted from the surface.*

PIPING 'SNAIL TRAILS' OR SHAPED TRAIL TRIMS AND LINES

Royal icing is perfect for piping trims around the base of cake tiers, around top edges or around sugar details, to enhance the design and hide joins. 'Snail trails' can be made using different nozzles, including a round, shell or star nozzle, to create alternative finishes. See the Wedgwood-Inspired White-on-White Wedding Cake (see page 72).

To create a joined-up 'snail trail', use stiff-peak royal icing in a piping bag with a No. 2 or No. 3 nozzle, depending on the size of the pearls or gap on your cake or board. Begin at the back of

your cake or at a convenient starting point if you are framing an image or sugar design. Pipe a pearl with gentle pressure, then release the pressure on the bag and draw the nozzle away from the pearl to create a little tail on the surface of the cake or iced board. Pipe another pearl, just slightly overlapping that tail, to start the trail. Continue all around the cake or design until you have a gorgeous sugar-pearl trail frame.

PIPING PEARL BEADS:

You can use these delicate iced pearls for all sorts of designs, or pipe them next to each other to create the effect of a bead trim; it has a different look to a 'snail trail', more like a string of spherical pearls than a joined up 'trail'. Paint dry pearls with pearl or metallic lustres mixed with rejuvenator spirit or piping gel and they look like edible jewellery!

To pipe an individual trail of simple pearl beads, use a No. 3 nozzle and pipe directly onto the surface of your cake or board, facing straight on. Squeeze the piping bag until your pearl is the desired size (I like them about 5 mm/¼ in diameter); when you are happy with the size, stop pressing and pull the nozzle quickly away from the iced pearl. You might get a tiny 'tail' or 'snag' when you pull the nozzle away from the pearl (we call them 'nipples' in the trade). If you do, just use a small paintbrush dampened with some cooled boiled water and, after you've piped a few pearls, press them lightly with the brush on the peaked bit. It will then sit flush into the pearl.

PIPING PATTERNS TO TEXTURISE ICING

FILIGREE PIPING

Simple filigree is really just squiggly, swirly lines in groups and patterns, applied free-hand using soft-peak royal icing. Once the whole cake is iced, it looks lovely. Google 'filigree icing patterns' and have a go.

TIP › *When new to icing, it's always a good idea to practise on your work surface a few times to get the feel of working with the medium and practise your patterns before piping on the cake.*

LACE OR PATTERN PIPING

You may like to pipe a pattern on your cake (from an invite, perhaps, or a favourite picture). You can do this free-hand directly onto the cake. If you are a little nervous, trace the main parts with a scriber needle or use an impression pin on the icing and pipe over the pattern(s) to create a lace piped effect on the surface.

BRUSH EMBROIDERY

Brush embroidery is a great way to enhance lace piping. After piping out a shape – lace floral ones work particularly well – use a small, damp artist's brush (a No. 3 or 4), to gently press on to the outer edges of the piping and draw the brush inwards. The more intricate your pattern, the smaller the brush you will need. It creates an embroidered effect, with the pattern slightly raised at the outer edges. I used this technique on a vintage-style pattern for Fearne Cotton's 30th birthday cake and on the Vase & Flowers cake on page 27. The good thing about any of these piping patterns is that you can hide a multitude of sins on the cake surface, e.g. small lumps and bumps, or small holes and tears, if you aren't the best at covering.

NOTE

~~~

You can score a straight line to follow, by using a cake smoother as a guide

PRESSURE PIPING

This is a bit tricky, so it's worthwhile trying out some or all of the previous piping patterns to get a feel for it before having a go. With pressure piping, you vary the pressure as you push out the icing, leaving you with heavier, more pronounced parts throughout the design, and thinner trails where you have tailed off the pressure. This is all done by hand. It has quite a regal and old-fashioned look and it's a bit dated at the moment, but these things come back and you may like to try it for a particular cake or idea – it's very old-school!

A simple pressure-piping technique is to create little piped hearts on a cake, which make for lovely 'fillers' to pipe over a cake's surface. Use a piping bag filled with soft-peak royal icing and fitted with a No. 3 nozzle, and apply pressure to extrude a bead, then release the pressure whilst dragging back. This creates a pearl with a tail trailing off. Pipe another bead right up next to the first bead and drag away the nozzle again. This creates a simple piped heart effect, and is a good introduction to the art of pressure piping.

If you want to try a structured pressure-piped design, mark out the pattern onto the sides of your cake rather than do it free-hand, making sure you measure the edges then space the different patterns evenly around your cake.

LINEA OR 'CANDY STRIPE' PIPING

This is one of the more tricky cake decorating techniques, but it's very eye-catching, particularly if you use a few different colours or shades. The sugary lines dropping straight down around the sides of the cake look very pretty. If you're new to it, practice on a blank cake dummy first, or an upturned cake tin, so that you can get a feel for it. It helps if you have a steady hand.

You can cover small or large cakes with candy stripes; on small cakes start right at the centre of the top of the cake; on large cakes, score a line around the top of your cake tier with a cake drum 2.5 cm (1 in) smaller than your cake – this will be your guide for where you start piping each line from. Sit mini bite-sized cakes on a square of greaseproof paper, so that when the icing is dry, you can carefully peel away the paper and will be left with a neat stripe design that finishes right at the bottom. If you did this onto a board, then tried to move it when wet, the icing would get messy when you pull it off the board. Or it would possibly crack if it had dried. Make sure large cakes are stuck fast on a cake board or iced cake tier.

Fill a piping bag fitted with a No. 3 nozzle with soft-peak royal icing and bring the nozzle up close to the cake. Squeeze the bag with light pressure so the icing begins to flow out. (It helps if you do this on a turntable but it's not essential.) Pipe a straight line all the way down the side of the cake, allowing the icing to flow out of the nozzle while you lift the bag away from the cake. Let gravity to pull the icing down. When you are almost at the bottom, bring your nozzle close into the cake and at the bottom stop squeezing and pull away. Remove little 'tails' if you get them.

RECIPES

Sponges, cookies, fillings
& coverings

VANILLA BEAN SPONGE

This is a classic, simple recipe: equal quantities of everything. You can use it to make cupcakes or bake it in large tins for celebration cakes. I make it extra gorgeous by adding plenty of vanilla bean paste and vanilla syrup once it's baked (which also prolongs its shelf-life).

The way we use our sponge mixes at Fancy Nancy is by weight of the total batter for a tin (see pages 162–63: most cakes in this book are made with two cakes sandwiched together. Refer to the weight of the total mix or tin sizes that I have used for each individual project if the project uses vanilla sponge cake. (The Rich Fruit Cake is an exception to this rule, as it is just baked in one tin – see page 211 for guide.)

You can change the sizes of the cake projects to suit your needs by using smaller or larger tins, but ideally make each main cake/tier out of two separately-baked sponges for anything bigger than a 15 cm (6 in) cake, filling each tin just over halfway up (based on a standard 8 cm-/3 in-deep tin that I use, rather than baking one deeper sponge and splitting it in half to fill it).

This recipe can be multiplied as needed. A simple sponge mix is always 1 medium egg (approx. 50 g/2 oz), and 50 g (2 oz) each of butter, sugar and flour. So, for example, if I need a total of 800 g (1 lb 12 oz) of mix, that will be 200 g (7 oz) egg, so a four-egg mix plus 200 g (7 oz) each of butter, sugar and flour. Multiply the four-egg mixture as required. If you have more than you need, you can always make the cakes a little deeper and cut them down, or just make a few extra cupcakes and freeze them or decorate them to go with your main cake.

You can add other flavours (see Variations on page 204), too. I customised this basic recipe for a fab Deep South-theme birthday cake for Bob and Pixie Geldof, lacing the syrup and caramel buttercream with Southern Comfort. And I used absinth in some fondant cupcakes for Marilyn Manson once, as you do!

〰〰〰

NOTE › *For cupcakes, I use muffin-sized cupcake cases. If you are using larger or smaller cases, adjust quantities as necessary. I fill cupcake cases half full if I'm going to be covering them with buttercream, and a third full if covering with fondant or ganache that I want to sit fairly flat. I have discovered some really fun edible wafer cupcake cases, from Dr. Oetker, which don't require a cupcake tin (see page 224 for stockists).*

(Recipe overleaf). →

TOP TIP

~~~

Have all your ingredients
at room temperature. If
your ingredients are cold
they will not combine
well and the eggs
may curdle.

FOR THE VANILLA SOAKING SYRUP AND VANILLA BEAN SPONGE

Make the syrup before you bake your sponge. It will keep in the fridge for up to one week, or can be frozen. This recipe makes enough syrup to brush and soak the tops of about 30 cupcakes. If you are making hundreds of cupcakes for a big party, multiply as necessary. For larger sponges, take the cakes out of their tins, brush them all over the bottom, then flip them over and skewer the domed top and brush generously with the syrup. **Makes 12–16 cupcakes or a 15 cm (6 in) cake**

STUFF YOU'LL NEED

Prep: 15 minutes for the syrup, 20 minutes for the cake
Cook: 10–15 minutes for the cupcake; larger cake tins will vary

TIP › *if you want to make a tall celebration cake, double thr quantities to half-fill two 15 cm/6 in round tins*

Equipment:
› 2 x 12-hole muffin trays and 16 cupcake cases (or a 15 cm/ 6 in round cake tin)

› cupcake cases or baking parchment
› microwaveable bowl or small saucepan
› spoon
› mixing bowl or stand mixer
› knife or metal skewer
› wire cooling rack
› silicone pastry brush

Ingredients:
For the vanilla soaking syrup:
› 100 g (3½ oz/scant ½ cup) golden caster (superfine) sugar

› 100 ml (3½ fl oz) just-boiled water
› seeds scraped from 1 split vanilla pod, or 2 teaspoons vanilla bean paste

For the vanilla bean sponge
› 200 g (7 oz) salted butter, at room temperature
› 200 g (7 oz/generous ¾ cup) golden caster (superfine) sugar
› seeds scraped from 1 split vanilla pod or 2 teaspoons vanilla bean paste

› 1 teaspoon good-quality vanilla extract
› 4 medium organic free-range eggs, lightly beaten
› 2 tablespoons soured cream or yogurt (optional – makes gluten-free sponges softer)
› 200 g (7 oz/1²/₃ cups) self-raising flour (or use 180 g/ 6 oz/scant
› 1½ cups self-raising or gluten-free flour

01. Preheat the oven to 180°C (350°F/Gas 4) and line the cupcake trays with cases or line the cake tin (see page 164).

02. To make the syrup, pop the sugar in a heatproof bowl or pan. Pour the water over the sugar. Place in the microwave for 1 minute at a time, stirring frequently, until the sugar has dissolved. Or, on the hob, stir gently over a low heat (do not boil) until all the sugar has dissolved and you have a syrupy liquid. Leave to cool for a few minutes then add the vanilla pod or paste and set aside to infuse.

03. To make the sponge, place the butter, sugar, vanilla seeds or paste and vanilla extract or flavourings (if using – see Variations on page 204) into a mixing bowl and beat until the mixture is very pale, soft and fluffy, and the granules of sugar have disappeared.

04. Add the beaten eggs, a quarter at a time. Mix in each addition until thoroughly combined, then gradually fold in the soured cream or yogurt (if using).

05. Add the flour gradually, mixing it in gently. Take care not to over-mix or beat too vigorously or the sponge can turn out a bit tough.

06. Spoon the mixture into the prepared tins or cupcake cases as required. Bake cupcakes for 12 minutes, then begin checking every few minutes. For larger cakes, begin checking each sponge after 20 minutes. The cake(s) should be a light golden brown, springy to the touch and a sharp knife or metal skewer inserted into the middle of the cake(s) should come out clean.

07. Once baked, transfer the cake(s) to a wire cooling rack. While still warm, brush the top of the cake(s) with a little of the vanilla or flavoured syrup using a silicone pastry brush, and brush the bottoms (removing the baking parchment first), then spear the top(s) in several places and brush or drizzle with syrup so the syrup can soak into the sponge. Leave the cakes to cool, then decorate or store as required.

A large cake will keep well for up to five days. You can also freeze the sponge (double-wrapped in cling film and store in a freezer bag) or you can split and fill it on its cake drum, then chill it to firm up, then double wrap and bag, and freeze for up to 1 month. To defrost, take out and allow to come to room temperature, ideally overnight.

SYRUP VARIATIONS

CITRUS SYRUP
Make the syrup lemony by using half and half fresh lemon juice and water, or the same for orange, along with some grated zest. You can also add orange or lemon oil to taste, or some Grand Marnier (lovely in an orange syrup) or limoncello (in a lemon syrup).

CARAMEL SYRUP
Make a darker caramel syrup by using a light muscovado sugar, or add a bit of booze, to taste, for example some whisky or Southern Comfort.

SPONGE VARIATIONS

LEMON/ORANGE SPONGE
Add the grated zest of two unwaxed lemons or the zest of two oranges. To enhance the flavour further, soak with your flavoured syrup (with or without alcohol).

FRUIT SPONGE
Add fresh fruits to the sponge for a light summery cake, e.g. flour-dusted blueberries and raspberries, or freeze-dried fruits. (Note: sponges containing fruit don't freeze well.)

CARAMEL SPONGE
Add 1 tablespoon of black treacle to the sponge mixture and a two handfuls of baking fudge pieces at the end of step 5, with the flour. Fill the cake with a caramel buttercream, with a drizzle of extra caramel and sea salt (see buttercream recipes on page 219).

NOTE › *Iced cupcakes keep well for 3–4 days. They can be frozen, too, but take care not to knock the cases. I freeze them in a corrugated cupcake box that has little cupcake-sized inserts to keep them in shape, I then wrap cling film around the outside of the box. I have found that even buttercream or meringue-buttercream cupcakes freeze perfectly well if done like this, for up to one month. Allow cakes to come to room temperature for around 3–4 hours or overnight. Larger cakes, double-wrapped in cling film and popped into a freezer bag, sealed, keep in the freezer for up to one month. Defrost overnight.*

CHOCOLATE CUPCAKE SPONGE

I love this recipe. It's rich and moist, and I use it all the time at my bakery. The secret is to slightly under-bake the cupcakes, so they are nice and fudgy. Brush them with some vanilla syrup as soon as they come out of the oven, for extra moisture, if you like. If you use gluten-free flour, just add a couple of extra tablespoons of soured cream to keep the cake soft. **Makes 12–16 cupcakes**

STUFF YOU'LL NEED

Prep: 20 minutes
Cook: 15–20 minutes

Equipment:
› 2 x 12-hole muffin trays and 16 cupcake cases

Ingredients:
› 170 g (6 oz) plain (bittersweet) chocolate chips or broken bars (70% cocoa solids)
› 200 g (7 oz) light muscovado sugar
› 170 g (6 oz) salted butter, softened
› 3 medium organic free-range eggs, plus 2 egg yolks
› 100 g (3½ oz) soured cream
› 1 teaspoon good-quality vanilla extract
› 150 g (5 oz) self-raising flour or a gluten-free blend
› 2 tablespoons cocoa powder
› sponge soaking syrup (see pages 202 and 204), optional

01. Preheat the oven to 180°C (350°F/Gas 4). Take two 12-hole muffin tins and line 16 of the holes with your cupcake cases.

02. Melt the chocolate, sugar and butter together in the microwave on medium power for 1 minute at a time, stirring at each minute interval. Alternatively, melt them in a heatproof bowl set over a pan of just-simmering water (bain marie) and leave to cool.

03. Whisk the eggs, soured cream and vanilla extract in a separate bowl.

04. Sift the flour and cocoa powder into another large bowl and combine with a spoon.

05. Add the egg mixture to the melted chocolate mixture and stir well.

06. Fold the flour mixture into the chocolate mixture until combined.

07. Spoon the batter evenly into the cupcake cases, just over half full. Bake for 15–20 minutes until just firm. A knife inserted into the middle of a cake should come out pasty but not wet when it's cooked (not dry, as with a vanilla sponge). Brush with syrup when hot, if you like, and leave to cool in the tray.

Once cool, finish them with the topping of your choice. I love using a chocolate buttercream with some cream cheese beaten into the topping to add a savoury hint.

VARIATIONS

COOKIES AND CREAM CUPCAKES
Make these 'cookies and cream' by adding one broken Oreo cookie into the bottom of the cupcake case, then top with an Oreo meringue buttercream (see page 221) and cookie to decorate.

ROCKY ROAD CUPCAKES
Add mini marshmallows, fudge pieces and biscuit to the cake mix and top with vanilla meringue buttercream (see page 221), mini marshmallows, crushed biscuit and a drizzle of caramel sauce. Decorate with chocolate or espresso buttercream, or pouring ganache (see page 222), when cool.

BELGIAN CHOCOLATE BROWNIE TORTE CAKE

This one really is to die for. It's fudgy and decadent, and really popular for weddings. I've recently been giving it a twist and making it a 'cookies and cream' flavour, which is hugely popular (it seems to be a big hit with men in particular). This recipe should be under-baked, and is definitely best baked in two separate tins. The cake will keep, well wrapped and at room temperature, for two weeks. It can frozen for up to three months if double-wrapped and sealed in a freezer bag. We use this cake to make all of our cake pops because it holds its shape when moulding without the need for additional buttercream. In fact, you could make balls from it for your Christmas Snowman Mini Cakes (see page 114), if you prefer chocolate. See chart on pages 162–63 for a guide to quantities for making larger cakes. **Makes 15 cm (6 in) cake**

STUFF YOU'LL NEED

Prep: 20 minutes
Cook: 30–40 minutes

Equipment:
› 2 x 15 cm (6 in) round tins
› Electric food mixer, with a

paddle or beater attachment

Ingredients:
› 6 medium organic free-range eggs
› 50 g (2 oz) soured cream
› 2 teaspoons vanilla extract

› 225 g (8 oz) plain bittersweet chocolate chips or broken bars (70% cocoa solids)
› 250 g (9 oz) unsalted butter, softened
› 350 g (12 oz/1¾ cups) light

muscovado sugar
› 225 g (8 oz/scant 2 cups) plain (all-purpose) flour (or a gluten-free flour blend)

---

01. Preheat the oven to 140°C (300°F/Gas 2) and line the tins with baking parchment.

02. Beat the eggs with the soured cream and vanilla extract and set aside, then melt the chocolate in the microwave on medium power for 1 minute at a time, stirring at each minute interval. Alternatively, melt it in a heatproof bowl set over a pan of just-simmering water (bain marie), and then leave to cool.

03. In a large bowl, beat the butter and sugar slowly by hand with a wooden spoon or in a stand mixer until combined, then increase the speed and continue to beat until the mixture is soft, pale and fluffy.

04. Add the beaten egg mixture a little at a time, mixing slowly until thoroughly incorporated.

05. Pour the cooled chocolate into the mixture, beating continuously until everything is combined.

06. Fold the flour into the mixture until just incorporated.

07. Spoon the batter evenly into the prepared tins and bake for 25 minutes. Check on the cakes every 5 minutes after this, removing them when they are well risen, but still wobble a bit when shaken (30–40 minutes); the crust will sink back into the cake as it cools. When cooked the knife or metal skewer inserted into the middle of the cakes should come out clean.

08. Remove the cakes from the oven and leave to cool in the tin. Sandwich together with the filling of your choice, trimming off the top crusts if you like, to leave a softer cake.

VARIATIONS

CHOCOLATE ORANGE CAKE
Use chocolate orange buttercream to sandwich the cake together.

COOKIES AND CREAM CAKE
Break six or seven Oreo cookies over the top of the mixture in each tin before baking, pressing the cookies down into the mix with the back of a metal spoon. Bake as above and, once cooled, sandwich the cake with some Oreo Crush Meringue Buttercream (see page 221).

RICH FRUIT CAKE

This is the best fruit cake recipe ever. It's delicious and doesn't need long to improve in flavour once baked. You could make it a few months in advance and keep it wrapped, feeding it occasionally with brandy, but if you make it just a couple of weeks before using it, it is still perfect. **Makes 15 cm (6 in) cake**

STUFF YOU'LL NEED

Prep: 15 mins
Cook: approx. 3 hours

Equipment:
› 15 cm (6 in) round tin
› baking parchment
› 2 x large mixing bowls
› wooden spoon
› small microwavable bowl or a small saucepan

Ingredients:
› 120 g (4 oz) sultanas
› 180 g (6 oz) raisins
› 180 g (6 oz) currants
› 50 g (2 oz) mixed peel
› 150 g (5 oz) natural-colour glacé cherries, washed and halved
› 100 g (3½ oz) salted butter
› 100 g (3½ oz/generous ¼ cup) molasses
› 2 organic free-range eggs
› 1 tablespoon vanilla extract
› ¼ teaspoon ground cinnamon
› ¼ teaspoon ground ginger
› ¼ teaspoon ground nutmeg
› pinch of ground cloves
› ¼ teaspoon mixed spice
› 90 g (3 oz/¾ cup) plain (all-purpose) flour or gluten-free flour blend (if using add ½ a beaten egg extra)
› 80 ml (3 fl oz) brandy, plus extra to feed cake (75–100 ml)
› 30 ml (1 fl oz) vodka

01. Preheat the oven to 140°C (275°F/Gas 1), and line the cake tin with baking parchment.

02. Place all the dried fruit, peel and glacé cherries in a large bowl big enough to hold the entire cake mix and combine with a large wooden spoon.

03. Melt the butter with the sugar in the microwave, stirring with a whisk at 1 minute intervals to mix the butter and sugar together. If you don't have a microwave, do this in a non-stick pan over a low heat and melt gently, stirring to mix.

04. Beat the eggs with the vanilla extract.

05. In a separate large bowl, combine the spices with the flour and mix well.

06. Tip the warm butter and sugar mix into the large bowl of dried fruit and mix well. Add the beaten egg, mixing well, followed by the flour and spice mix. Stir in until just combined. Finally, add the brandy and vodka.

07. Spoon the mixture into the prepared tin and bake for 1 hour, then turn the heat down to 125°C (250°F/Gas ½) and continue to bake until completely cooked through. The cake will take 2–2½ hours to cook, depending on your oven. Pay attention to the cake during the long cooking time and check it every 30 minutes or so; a sharp knife or skewer inserted into the middle of the cake should come out almost clean. (Much larger fruit cakes take longer. If I am making a large 30 cm (12 in) cake it takes 6–7 hours.)

08. Leave to cool, then brush with a little more brandy and double-wrap in baking parchment, followed by a layer of foil. Store for up to 6 months in a cool, dry place and its flavour will improve, but it can be used within a couple of weeks, too. It can also be frozen for up to two years if well-wrapped (to protect it from freezer burn). I have had several brides come back to me with their leftover wedding cake after a couple of years, and I've re-iced it for a christening cake! Check to taste before serving, and periodically feed with more brandy, if you wish.

~

To work out how much more mix you'll need for larger tins, fill a 15 cm (6 in) cake tin with water and measure the volume. For larger tins, fill these up first with water, then you can work out how many more times volume you needed from the 15 cm (6 in) cake tin amount, which will tell you how many times to multiply this cake mix by. I've included a guide chart as well.

I like to bake fruit cakes fairly deep, almost to the top of the tin, so as a guide for the following sizes allow for more uncooked fruit cake mix. As long as your tin isn't full to the top it is fine to add a little more or less mix; you will just get a different depth.

ROUND CAKE TINS

18 cm (7 in) 2 kg (4 lb 6 oz)
20 cm (8 in) 2.65 kg (5 lb 13½ oz)
23 cm (9 in) 3.35 kg (7 lb 6 oz)
25 cm (10 in) 3.9 kg (8 lb 9½ oz)
28 cm (11 in) 4.85 kg (10 lb 11 oz)
30 cm (12 in) 6.2 kg (13 lb 11 oz)

SQUARE CAKE TINS

(Square tins take more mix so add approx. 15% on for standard 7.5 cm-/3 in-deep tins, to allow for the corners.)
15 cm (6 in) 1.75 kg (3 lb 14 oz)
18 cm (7 in) 2.3 kg (5 lb 1 oz)
20 cm (8 in) 3 kg (6 lb 10 oz)
23 cm (9 in) 3.8kg (8 lb 6 oz)
25 cm (10 in) 4.45 kg (9 lb 13 oz)
28 cm (11 in) 5.5kg (12 lb 2 oz)
30 cm (12 in) 7.15 kg (15 lb 2 oz)

TOP TIP
〜
If you want to make the cookies into lollipops you'll need sticks (see page 224 for stockists)

VANILLA COOKIES

I've repeated this recipe, which appeared in my first book, because it's a lovely, easy cookie recipe: it tastes great, has a good crunch, and it is firm enough to work with and decorate elaborately. It rolls out well and you can re-roll it by just popping off-cuts back into your mixer and adding a little more beaten egg or a few drops of water. This is the recipe I use for cookie lollipops (great gifts or brilliant cake decorations) and my Tattooed Sailor Nautical Cookie Explosion cake (see page 36). The baked cookies will keep for 8–10 weeks, as long as they are well wrapped, making them perfect for wedding or party favours, teacher's pressies or promotional cookies for your own or a friend's business (what better way of spreading the word than an edible one!). **Makes approximately 20 cookies**

STUFF YOU'LL NEED

Prep: 10–15 minutes
Cook: 10–12 minutes

Equipment:
› 2 x baking sheets
› baking parchment
› mixing bowl
› wooden spoons or mixer with

paddle attachment
› rolling pin
› guide sticks (optional)
› palette knife
› cookie cutters or card templates
› sharp knife (optional)
› wire cooling rack

Ingredients:
› 200 g (7 oz) salted butter, softened
› 200 g (7 oz/generous ¾ cup) golden caster (superfine) sugar
› seeds scraped from 1 split vanilla pod or 2 teaspoons good-quality vanilla bean paste

› 1 organic free-range egg, lightly beaten
› 400 g (14 oz/1²/₃) plain (all-purpose) flour, sifted, plus extra for dusting

---

01. Preheat the oven to 180°C (350°F/Gas 4) and line two baking sheets with baking parchment.

~~~~~~

02. Place the butter and sugar along with the vanilla seeds or paste into a mixing bowl and mix until just combined, either by hand or using a stand mixer on a slow speed. Don't be tempted to beat it until creamy like you would a sponge mix, or your cookies will spread when baking. The mix should still look grainy but be thoroughly incorporated (use a spatula to make sure you get all the lumps from the side of your mixing bowl if you are using a stand mixer).

~~~~~~

03. Add the egg a little at a time, on a slow speed with your mixer or with a wooden spoon, until fully incorporated.

~~~~~~

04. Add the flour to the mixture and mix until a dough forms. If the mix is a little sticky, add a little more flour, or, alternatively, if it's a bit dry add a few drops of water. You will know it's right when the dough comes together without

leaving sticky traces on the bowl and it forms into a nice shiny pliable ball.

~~~~~~

05. Dust the work surface with flour and roll out the cookie dough. Place your rolling pin in the centre of the dough and roll away from your body, then bring the pin back to the centre and roll towards yourself. Turn a quarter turn, sweeping some flour under the dough and repeat. Using guide sticks will ensure your dough is an even thickness, a foolproof way to make sure you get an even bake and a neater cookie. If you don't have guide sticks, just take care to apply even pressure, and roll to a thickness of about 5 mm (¼ in). This will ensure all the cookies bake evenly.

~~~~~~

06. Cut out your shapes with your chosen cookie cutter(s) or use a card template (see pages 226–29 for templates, which you can trace and stick to a piece of card). Place the template on top of the rolled-out dough and cut around it with a sharp knife. →

~~~~~~

07. Pick up your cookies with a palette knife or thin cake slice and place them on the prepared baking sheets. If you are using lollipop sticks, push them into the cookie dough once the cookies are on the baking sheet: carefully push the stick up through the middle, without it cracking the top. Push it in just over halfway up the shape. Don't worry if you end up with breakages, it's easy to re-roll the dough.

~~~~~~~~~~

08. Bake for 10–12 minutes for small–medium sized cookies, checking after 10 minutes as all ovens vary and you may need to give them a few more minutes. The cookies should be golden brown, firm and springy to the touch. Cool on a wire rack and then decorate as required.

VARIATIONS

FESTIVE SPICE

(I made this lovely recipe for a Christmas cake idea for *Delicious* magazine; it's a gorgeous lighter option to gingerbread.) Add 1 teaspoon ground ginger, 1½ teaspoons ground cinnamon and a good pinch of mixed spice to the plain flour. Sift together then follow method from page 213.

CITRUS

Add the grated zest of two unwaxed lemons or oranges to the butter and sugar.

CHOCOLATE

Replace 20 g (¾ oz) of the flour with 20 g (¾ oz) cocoa powder.

MOCHA

Replace 30 g (1 oz) of the flour with 15 g (½ oz) espresso powder and 15 g (½ oz) cocoa powder.

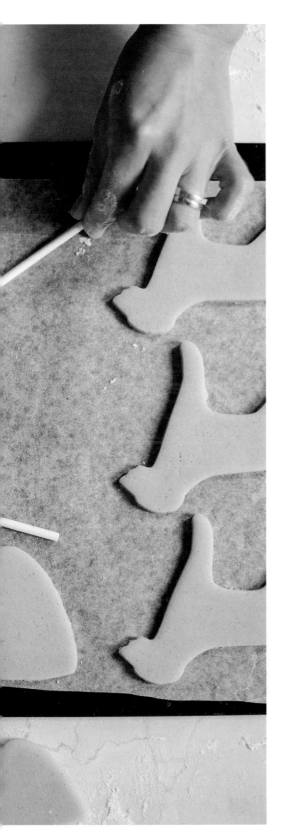

GINGERBREAD COOKIE DOUGH

I love this recipe; it's delicious and very authentic. The baked cookies will keep for up to 12 weeks, if kept well wrapped. You can also make the dough in advance and freeze it or keep it in the fridge for a few days before rolling out, cutting and baking. I've used this in my Christmas Kitsch Cookies (see page 122).
Makes approximately 24 cookies

STUFF YOU'LL NEED

Equipment:
› saucepan
› wooden spoons or mixer with paddle attachment
› cling film

Ingredients:
› 70 g (2¼ oz) golden syrup
› juice of 1 orange
› 90 g (3 oz/½ cup) light muscovado sugar
› 1 tablespoon ground ginger
› 2 teaspoons ground cinnamon
› 100 g (3½ oz) salted butter, diced
› 1 teaspoon vanilla bean paste
› 1 scant teaspoon bicarbonate of soda (baking soda)
› 240 g (8½ oz/2 scant cups) plain (all-purpose) flour

01. Put the golden syrup, orange juice, muscavado sugar, ginger and cinnamon into a saucepan and heat until it has melted. Don't let the mixture boil or it will make your cookies tough. Stir constantly.

02. Once the sugar has dissolved, add the butter and vanilla paste. Stir gently until melted and incorporated into the warm sugar mix.

03. Add the bicarbonate of soda and whisk it in to the warm sugar and butter mix with a metal whisk until fluffy and paler in colour.

04. Tip the mixture into the bowl of a stand mixer or a mixing bowl and, when cooled, gradually add the flour and beat on a slow speed or mix with a wooden spoon until the mixture comes together and resembles an oily dough.

05. Turn out onto two large pieces of cling film laid out in a cross formation and wrap up to seal the block of dough. Chill for at least two hours before rolling, and cutting into shapes, or leave overnight in the fridge and roll out the next day. The dough can be frozen for up to one month. To defrost, place in the fridge overnight then leave out at room temperature for 1 hour and knead the dough until pliable.

VANILLA BEAN BUTTERCREAM

This basic buttercream is really easy to make, and is perfect for large cakes; it has a stiff consistency and sets well. Use the best possible ingredients you can, ideally natural unrefined icing (confectioners') sugar, as it has a lovely caramel quality (only for use inside cakes though; if you want a whiter finish, use regular white icing sugar). For cupcakes, I tend to soften the buttercream with a little cream cheese, or for the ultimate cupcake buttercream (which I really love to use on the Cupcake Bouquet on page 33) I make the amazing Meringue Buttercream (see page 221). **Fills and covers a 15 cm (6 in) round cake**

STUFF YOU'LL NEED

Prep: 10 mins

Equipment:
› stand mixer with beater or paddle attachment or electric hand-held mixer or wooden spoon
› tea towel (optional)

Ingredients:
› 250 g (9 oz) unsalted butter, softened
› 2 teaspoons good-quality vanilla extract
› seeds scraped from 1 split vanilla pod (save the pod for syrups or put in your sugar jar) or 2 teaspoons vanilla bean paste
› 500 g (1 lb 2 oz/4 cups) natural unrefined icing (confectioners') sugar, sifted

(if you are using inside a cake, use unrefined; for covering a cake, use white sugar)

---

01. In a stand mixer with the beater or paddle attachment (or in a bowl using a hand-held electric mixer or wooden spoon), cream the butter with the vanilla extract and seeds or paste until very pale, soft and smooth.

02. Add about a quarter of the icing sugar. Mix slowly at first (so the sugar doesn't puff out all over the kitchen), using a tea towel over the bowl if you are worried about it spilling out of the mixer bowl. Once it is all mixed in, beat the sugar into the butter for about 1 minute on the fast speed, or with plenty of elbow grease and a wooden spoon, until the mixture is really creamy and pale. It will take you a few minutes if mixing by hand.

03. Continue adding the sugar in three more increments, taking care to beat it in completely at each addition.

04. Finally, beat the buttercream on the fast speed for a minute or two until it's fluffy and pale.

VARIATIONS

ORANGE BUTTERCREAM

Follow the basic vanilla buttercream recipe, but when you cream the butter, add the grated zest of two oranges. You can, of course, still use the vanilla – it works well with the orange – but omit it if you prefer. For a bit of naughtiness, add a splash of Grand Marnier if you like.

FRESH RASPBERRY AND STRAWBERRY BUTTERCREAM

Follow the basic vanilla buttercream recipe, but add 4 tablespoons of the following simple fruit coulis to give the buttercream a fresh, fruity kick. A great combination is to split a vanilla sponge twice and add a layer of vanilla and a layer of the berry buttercream (it look really appealing when cut, and tastes amazing).

01. Rinse one 200 g (7 oz) punnet of fresh raspberries and one 200 g (7 oz) punnet of fresh strawberries, hulled, and blend them to a purée in a food processor or using a hand blender. Pass the purée through a sieve into a small saucepan.

02. Bring the purée to a gentle boil over a low heat and reduce the fruity liquid for about 5 minutes until its volume has halved. Leave to cool. This can be kept in the fridge for a few days or frozen. →

03. Add about 4 tablespoons of the fruity paste to the vanilla buttercream. If you want to cheat a strawberry or berry filling, just stir in some good-quality jam to taste. I do love the Tiptree Little Scarlett jam – it's fab and I'm not biased at all, being from Essex.

LEMON BUTTERCREAM

Follow the basic vanilla buttercream recipe, but add the grated zest of two unwaxed lemons and 100 g (3½ oz) of home-made or shop-bought lemon curd. Add a dash of limoncello for an extra kick, if you like.

BELGIAN CHOCOLATE GANACHE BUTTERCREAM:

This will give you a perfect buttercream that's ideal for filling the Belgian Chocolate Brownie Torte Cake (see page 209) or the Vanilla Bean Sponge (see page 200). It can also be used to cover cakes. Add some cream cheese to taste if you want to top cupcakes with this recipe.

1. Place 75 ml (2½ fl oz) double (heavy) cream (organic if possible) and 150 g (5 oz) good-quality Belgian chocolate, minimum 70% cocoa solids (chips or a bar broken into small chunks), into a microwaveable bowl and heat on medium power for 1 minute at a time, stirring at minute intervals, until the chocolate has melted into the cream and you have a smooth velvety ganache. Alternatively, melt it in a heatproof bowl over a pan of gently simmering water (bain marie). Leave to cool.

2. Once cooled, stir the ganache into the buttercream. Be sure it's completely cool, or the ganache will split the mixture and make your buttercream oily.

SALTED CARAMEL BUTTERCREAM

This is Lydia and Ruby's favourite topping; they love the Sea Salted Caramel Seaside Cupcakes (see page 99). Follow the basic vanilla buttercream recipe, using unrefined icing sugar, but stir in 3 large tablespoons of good-quality caramel (the Callebaut brand is lovely) and beat in well. Add 150 g (5 oz) cream cheese and beat it in slowly to incorporate. Once you have filled the cake, add a drizzle of caramel over the filling and sprinkle with flakes of sea salt, or, if piping onto cupcakes, drizzle each one with a swirl of caramel and add a sprinkling of the crunchy salt flakes to each cake.

Alternatively, make your own caramel. See opposite for my preferred recipe.

TOP TIP

~~~

Adding a little cream cheese to any buttercream will improve the eating quality and keep it slightly softer. I find it takes the edge off the sweetness of a buttercream.

HOMEMADE SALTED CARAMEL SAUCE

The thought of making caramel can be scary, but like anything, it will get easier with practice. Keep in mind a few tips when making this; stir the sugar initially to help it to melt evenly, but stop once it has completely melted or it can seize up. It is handy to use a sugar (candy) thermometer to make it easier to see the right point to add in the other stuff. The melted sugar should reach 170°C (340°F) on this. If you don't have one, here is what you should look for: the caramel should be a deep amber colour and should have only just started to smoke. If you don't cook it long enough it will be too sweet with little depth of flavour, but cook it too long and it will taste burnt. Once you've done it a few times you'll be able to tell without the thermometer and you'll be 'in tune' with your caramel creation! Use a saucepan that is fairly large because when you add the butter and the cream, the caramel will bubble up loads and it is extremely hot, it will bubble quite vigorously.
Makes approximately 700 ml (23½ fl oz) or two standard jam jars

STUFF YOU'LL NEED

Prep: approx. 15 minutes

Equipment:
› Heavy-based saucepan
› Wooden mixing spoon
› Sugar (candy) thermometer (optional)
› 2 x jam jars, sterilised

Ingredients:
› 400 g (14 oz) unrefined golden caster sugar
› 180 g (6 oz) unsalted butter cut into small chunks
› 250 g (9 oz) double cream
› 2 teaspoons of good-quality chunky sea salt flakes

01. Heat the sugar in an even layer in heavy-based saucepan, with a capacity of at least 2 litres (2½ pints) over a medium-high heat, stirring it as it begins to melt. The sugar will begin to form clumps, but just keep stirring and as it continues to cook. Stop mixing once all of the sugar has melted, and swirl the pan occasionally while the sugar cooks.

02. Continue cooking until the sugar has reached a deep amber colour and you can smell the toasty sugary caramel scent. Be careful not to burn it though! Once the temperature hits 170°C (340°F) it is ready.

03. Now add the butter all at once. Be careful, as the caramel will bubble up. Stir the butter into the caramel until it is completely melted.

04. Remove the saucepan from the heat and slowly pour the cream into the caramel taking care as it will still splutter. Whisk until all of the cream has been incorporated and you have a smooth sauce.

05. Add salt and mix thoroughly. Leave to cool for 10–15 minutes and then pour into a sterilised glass jam jars and let it cool to room temperature.

06. You can refrigerate the sauce for up to three weeks, but you'll need to warm it slightly to liquefy up before using. This is lovely beaten into cream cheese buttercream for the Sea Salted Caramel Cupcakes on page 99); beat in to taste (I like quite a lot!) This yields a large amount; you can also heat this in a plastic piping bag and drizzle over cakes and cupcakes as shown in the recipe.

MERINGUE BUTTERCREAM

*This recipe is a little long-winded but it's so worth it. It's easy to pipe with and has a light, almost custardy taste, so is not sickly sweet. And you don't get that crystalised, crusty top that you get from regular buttercream when it is exposed to the air – it stays soft. It is best used fresh, when you need it, though it stays beautifully soft on cupcakes for a few days. You can flavour it with strawberry fruit paste or coulis, but don't add too much as it can become too runny. Being a meringue recipe, it is absolutely vital that all of your equipment is clean and grease free. Use a stand mixer with whisk attachment if you have one. It is possible to make it by hand, but it will take longer. This is perfect for the Cupcake Bouquet (see page 33) or a collection of piped rose cupcakes on a plate using the large petal nozzle. **Covers 18–20 cupcakes***

STUFF YOU'LL NEED

Prep: 30 minutes, including cooling time if using a stand mixer

Ingredients:
› 160 g (5½ oz) egg white (you can find little cartons of pasteurised egg white in the supermarket) I favour the twochicks brand (see stockists page 224)
› 350 g (12 oz/2¾ cups) icing (confectioners') sugar
› 300 g (10½ oz) unsalted butter, at room temperature
› 2 teaspoons vanilla bean paste or seeds split from 2 scraped vanilla pods

01. Combine the egg whites and icing sugar in a spotlessly clean mixing bowl or the metal mixing bowl from your stand mixer and set over a pan of just-simmering water (making sure the bowl doesn't touch the water).

02. Whisk constantly by hand until the mixture is warm to the touch. The mixture should feel completely smooth, warm and silky when rubbed between your fingers. The sugar should be completely dissloved.

03. Leave to cool a little. You can place the hot bowl into some cold water if you wish, to speed up this process, but make sure no water splashes into the mix. Attach the bowl to the mixer fitted with the whisk attachment or just do the next bit by hand with a whisk and plenty of elbow grease.

04. Starting on a low speed, gradually increasing to medium-high speed, whisk the mixture until stiff (but not dry) peaks form and you have a glossy meringue consistency. Continue mixing until the mixture is fluffy and completely cool (test by touching the bottom of the bowl).

05. With mixer on a low speed, add the butter in small pieces, until it's all incorporated. Turn the speed to high and whip up until the mixture comes together as a lovely light and creamy frosting. It looks like it's curdling and separating just before it comes together so don't worry. Add the vanilla paste or seeds and then turn to a low speed to beat out some of the air. Colour with liquid colours and pipe away.

VARIATION

OREO CRUSH

This cookies and cream topping is truly scrumptious. You can use it to fill and crumb-coat large cakes (it works perfectly with the Belgian Chocolate Brownie Torte Cake with Oreos baked in the sponge – see page 209) or top cupcakes. This is a big hit with the boys, it's George's favourite ever cake!

To transform the buttercream into a cookies and cream topping, take one pack of Oreo cookies and whizz them in a food processor to fine crumbs. (Make sure that they're whizzed thoroughly if you are piping on your cupcakes, so your nozzle doesn't become blocked.) Stir the crumbs into the meringue buttercream.

CHOCOLATE POURING GANACHE

This is DEAD easy, and so delicious. This is the recipe that my son George uses on his 'World's Best Dad Chocolate Mini Bites' on page 88, to which he added a dash of my husband Simon's favourite whisky. Other flavours work well, too. I love adding Nielsen-Massey orange oil to make this into a chocolate orange topping at Christmas that goes on a Grand Marnier-spiked orange sponge (see variation on page 204), making chocolate orange ganache cupcakes that are like grown-up Jaffa Cakes! The ganache can be frozen for up to one month or kept in the fridge for one week (it cools to a firmer, pipeable consistency). **Covers 16–20 mini-bites with extra to spare**

STUFF YOU'LL NEED

Prep: 10 minutes

Ingredients:
› 125 ml (4 fl oz) double (heavy) cream
› 500 g (1 lb 2 oz) good-quality dark chocolate chips or broken-up bars (70% cocoa solids)
› 250 g (9 oz) unsalted butter

01. Place all the ingredients in a microwaveable bowl and heat for 1 minute at a time, stirring at each interval, until all of the chocolate is melted and you are left with a velvety pourable ganache. Alternatively, melt it in a heatproof bowl set over a pan of just-simmering water (bain marie).

02. Allow to cool, adding a dash of booze, if you wish, and it's ready to pour over your cake(s). Yum!

BELGIAN WHITE CHOCOLATE ROLL-OUT PASTE

This is the easiest recipe I have found – a basic mix of thick syrup and white chocolate. I make it using a microwave, but if you do not have a microwave, melt the chocolate and warm the syrup in separate heatproof bowls set over a pan of just-simmering water (bain marie). This paste, which can be coloured by kneading in paste colour, is perfect for covering chocolate-decorated cakes, but is not stable enough for making larger structural decorations (i.e. in the Club Tropicana design – see page 126). For a milk or dark chocolate version, follow the same method below, but use just 180 ml (6 fl oz) corn syrup.
Makes approximately 1.25 kg (2 lb 12 oz) paste

STUFF YOU'LL NEED

Prep: 30 mins

Ingredients:
› 1 kg (2 lb 3 oz) good-quality white chocolate chips or broken-up bars
› 250 ml (8½ fl oz) light Karo corn syrup

01. Place the white chocolate in a microwaveable bowl and microwave on medium power for 30 seconds at a time, checking and stirring the chocolate at each interval, until completely melted. Do not overheat it, as white chocolate melts at a low temperature. If using a bain marie, be sure to melt it very gently.

02. Place the corn syrup in a separate microwaveable bowl and microwave on high power for 45 seconds (or heat gently in a bain marie until it reaches body temperature).

03. Pour the warmed syrup into the bowl of melted chocolate and stir together with a rubber spatula or wooden spoon until just amalgamated. Keep stirring for about 30 seconds until everything has come together and formed an oily mass (do not over-beat, or it can become too oily and split). Mix until all the white chocolate has disappeared or you may end up with hard bits of solid chocolate when you roll it out.

04. Scoop the warm paste immediately into a large food bag and press out any creases in the bag so that it clings tightly to the paste. If you leave creases in the bag they become trapped in the paste while cooling and you may find it tricky to get the plastic bag off without leaving some embedded in the hardened paste. Leave to set at room temperature overnight; it will solidify.

05. The paste is now ready to be used as a coating. Knead small chunks of it until it's warm and pliable, then roll out as you would sugarpaste or marzipan. It can be coloured by kneading in paste colour as you would with marzipan or sugarpaste (see page 177). If you find it too hard you can warm it for a few seconds at a time in the microwave to soften it a little. It will keep in a food bag for up to three months, or in the freezer for up to one year.

STOCKISTS & SUPPLIERS

CAKE & COOKIE DECORATING & BAKING SUPPLIES

UK
WWW.CAKEBOSS.CO.UK
WWW.SQUIRES-SHOP.COM
WWW.CAKE-STUFF.COM
WWW.ALMONDART.COM
WWW.CAKESCOOKIESANDCRAFTSSHOP.CO.UK
WWW.CRAFTMILL.CO.UK (*POLYSTYRENE BALLS*)
WWW.EBAY.CO.UK
WWW.AMAZON.CO.UK

US
WWW.CARLOSBAKERY.COM
WWW.USCAKE.COM
WWW.EBAY.COM
WWW.AMAZON.COM
WWW.SHOPBAKERSNOOK.COM

AUS
WWW.CUPIDSCAKEDECORATIONS.COM.AU
WWW.COMPLETECAKEDEC.CO.AU

EDIBLE PAINTS & GLITTERS

Rainbow Dust Colours Ltd
WWW.RAINBOWDUST.CO.UK
(US AND AUS MARKETS TRY EBAY OR AMAZON)

EDIBLE PRINT DESIGNS OR PARTY STATIONERY

Digital designs for edible prints
WWW.FRANCIS-DEE.CO.UK
WWW.HELLOLOVEDDESIGNS.COM
WWW.FANCYFLOURS.COM
WWW.CULPITTCAKECLUB.COM
(US AND AUS MARKETS TRY ETSY)

Edible printer supplies/sheets
WWW.DECO.UK.COM

INGREDIENTS (MY PREFERRED SUGARS, FLAVOURINGS & FLOURS)

Billington's (*their unrefined sugars give my bakes a rich molasses flavour – it makes such a difference*)
WWW.BILLINGTONS.CO.UK

Nielsen-Massey (*their vanilla extract, bean paste and pods give wonderful depth of flavour*)
WWW.NIELSENMASSEY.CO.UK

Allinson (*for flour*)
WWW.ALLINSONFLOUR.CO.UK

twochicks (*pasteurised liquid egg white*)
WWW.TWOCHICKS.CO.UK

Renshaw (*icing and marzipan*)
WWW.RENSHAWBAKING.COM

Dr. Oetker products, available in supermarkets
(*for marzipan, icings, edible cupcake cases and decorations*)
WWW.OETKER.CO.UK

Slovley Salt
WWW.SLOVLEY.CO.UK

Piran Salt
WWW.PIRANSALT.COM

Maldon Salt
WWW.MALDONSALT.CO.UK

CAKE & COOKIE PACKAGING

Keylink
WWW.KEYLINK.ORG

RIBBONS & TRIMMINGS

Mansell Ribbons
WWW.MANSELLRIBBONS.CO.UK

Also, special thanks to the following fabulous companies, who kindly supplied products and services for our photographs:

Shrinking Violet (*floristry*)
WWW.SHRINKINGVIOLETFLOWERS.COM

Rebecca Ryther Make-Up (*make-up and hair*) IAG
WWW.REBECCARYTHER.CO.UK

Cherrie Snow (*nail art*)
WWW.CHERRIESNOW.COM

KitchenAid (*props*)
WWW.KITCHENAID.CO.UK

Mason Cash (*props*)
WWW.MASONCASH.CO.UK

Chirs Wilson (*props*)
WWW.FOAMCUTTTING.CO.UK

Michelle Goldman (*fine artist*)
WWW.MICHELLEGOLDMAN.CO.UK

And a big thanks to **Marsh Farm** *for the hay!*
WWW.MARSHFARM.CO.UK

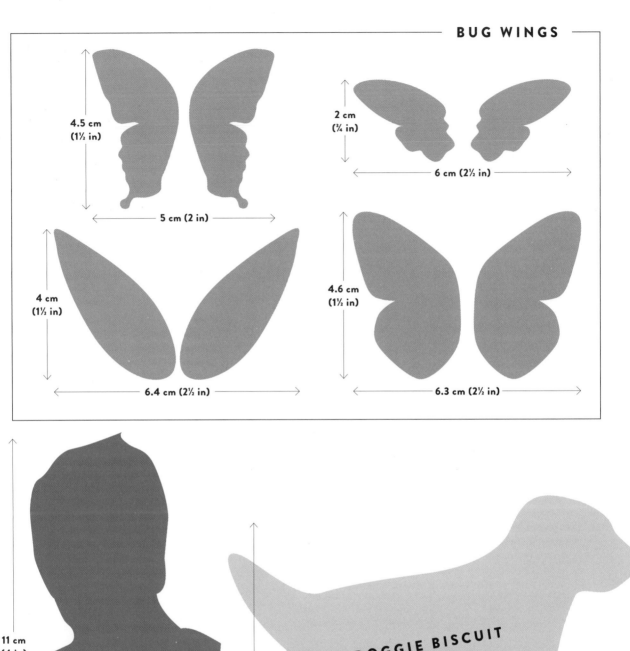

4.5 cm
(1½ in)

5 cm (2 in)

2 cm
(¾ in)

6 cm (2½ in)

4 cm
(1½ in)

6.4 cm (2½ in)

4.6 cm
(1½ in)

6.3 cm (2½ in)

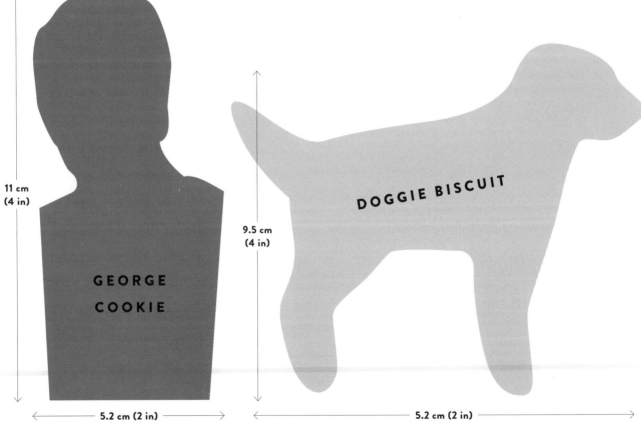

11 cm
(4 in)

GEORGE
COOKIE

5.2 cm (2 in)

9.5 cm
(4 in)

DOGGIE BISCUIT

5.2 cm (2 in)

LOVE HEART COOKIES

LOVE HEART
COOKIES

COOKIE
EXPLOSION
CAKE
(medium)

COOKIE
EXPLOSION CAKE
(large)

COOKIE
EXPLOSION
CAKE
(small)

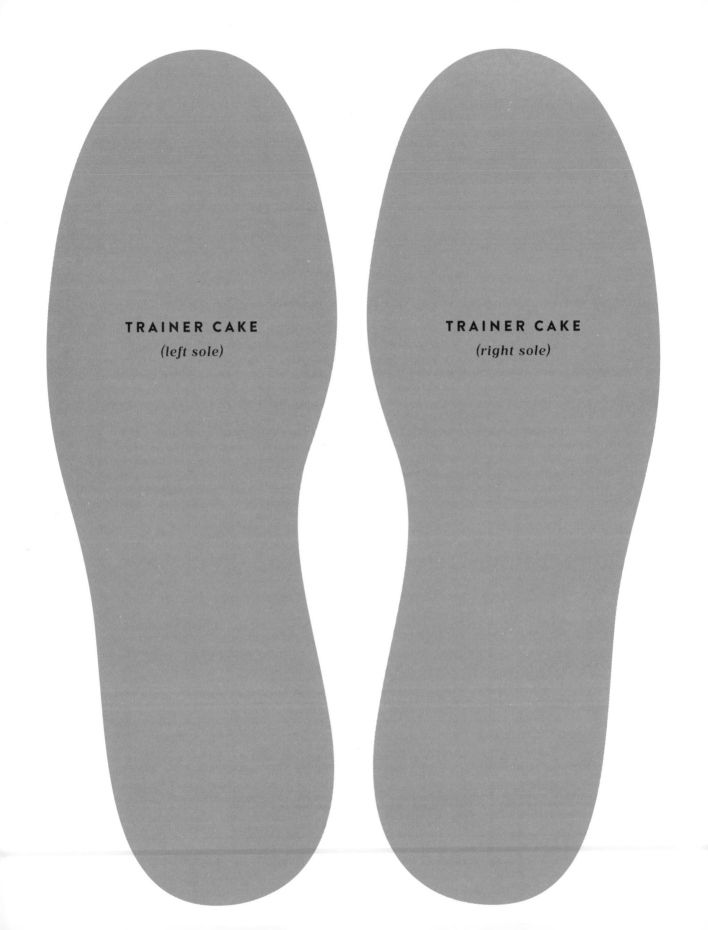

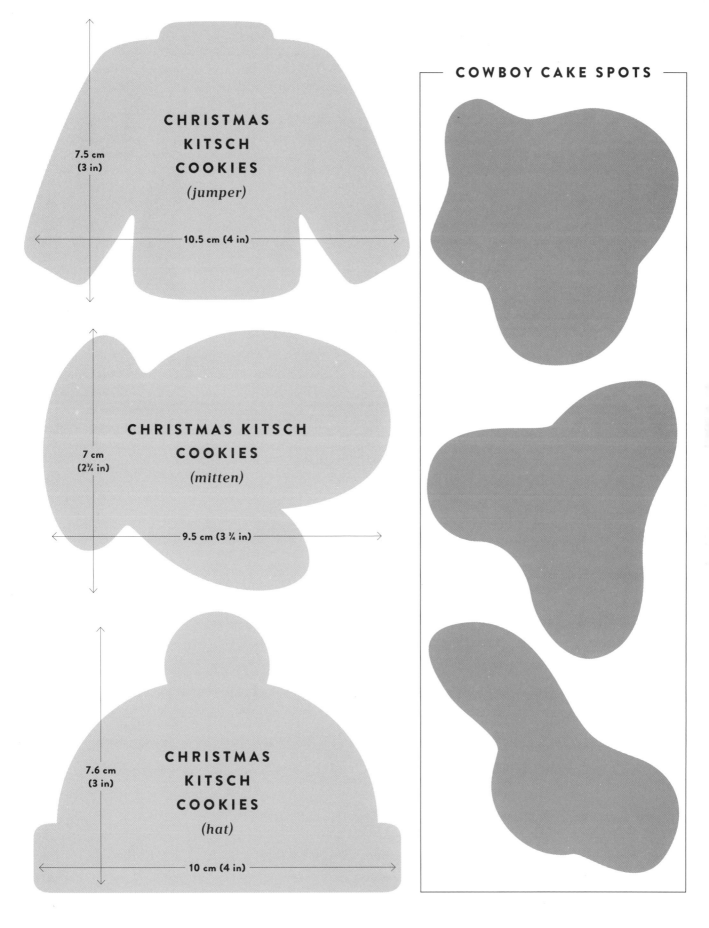

CHRISTMAS KITSCH COOKIES
(jumper)

7.5 cm (3 in)

10.5 cm (4 in)

CHRISTMAS KITSCH COOKIES
(mitten)

7 cm (2¼ in)

9.5 cm (3 ¾ in)

CHRISTMAS KITSCH COOKIES
(hat)

7.6 cm (3 in)

10 cm (4 in)

COWBOY CAKE SPOTS

THANK YOUS

I've absolutely loved writing and creating this book and there are so many people I would like to thank who have helped me along my merry cakey journey.

Firstly to Simon, thanks for encouraging and supporting me in every way and for living with ALL THE SUGAR MESS (especially during the shoot!) love you forever. BIG thanks to our gorgeous kids, Ruby, Lydia and George, for putting up with me working all the hours in the world and thanks for appearing in and creating stuff for the book, you are all brilliant.

To the rest of the family, thanks to Lydia, officially you are the best mother-in-law in the world for too many things, you are a legend and friend. Huge thanks to my dad George, engineer extraordinaire, cake gadget man and Super Grandad for all your help at the shop and at home as always. Sisterly love to 'the muse' Nancy, my fabulous sister and friend, for everything especially all the brilliant stylish props and decorations you make for us at the shop and for your help when the going gets tough. Thanks to Daisy and Delilah for

being supermodels for the book photoshoot, we all had fun and ate too many cakes and chocolate buttons!

Thanks to #teamfancynancyinternational we have a good old laugh despite the humungous work load, thanks for everything; to the fabulous Alison Penn, a true friend (creep), Lola Penn-Franzolin, Charlotte Fox, Lydia Sear junior and senior, George Walker, Milo Penn Franzolin, Tara Carter plus my freelance cakey pals Dan P Carter, Gemma Sisson and Roxanne Headland. Also to my teaching partner in crime, Christine Lee, you taught me everything I know about caking and are my bestest fwend. Thanks to Hsiu Ping Juan, who came to work with us from Taiwan, you are a superstar and were so helpful – sent to us like a sugary angel. Also to the lovely Qilu Xiao and Ying Hsin Hsu for helping the team with the book and running the bakery. Thanks to Jen Christie and Jane Graham Maw, my literary agents for your continued support, help and for singing my praises so passionately! Thanks to my super agents and friends Kim Farmer and Kirsty Williams.

Massive thanks to the wonderful team that have worked with me to produce this book, it's been so much fun! To the super talented Helen Cathcart for your AMAZING, AMAZING photography we had a great laugh and I am so elated with the photos, thanks for putting up with the chaos and of course your over-eager assistant Dolci the Dog during the shoot. AND for letting me and George come round to you and make even more mess at yours – I'm so glad I have met you. To my amazing Publisher, Kate, my wonderful Editor, Kajal, my brilliant Publicist, Emma and the rest of the Hardie Grant team; its been brilliant working with you all – you are all fantastic and have made the process creative, rewarding and so enjoyable. Thank you Laura Nickoll for all your help on the copy edit and Susan Pegg for your thorough proofread!

Thank you to the lovely April Carter for all your help on the shoot with the props, making tons of cakes, lists and buttercreams AND dealing with the cake bomb I produced everywhere in my wake. To Julia Murray huge thanks for your gorgeous design work I LOVE it – so clever!

Thanks to other fellow Leigh business peeps and great friends, Michelle Goldman for your brilliant art work, Lorraine and Nicky at Shrinking Violet for the beautiful flowers featured in the book, to Rebecca Ryther for your ace make up artist skills and to Cherrie Snow for the creative nail art, so cool!

Also huge thanks to some lovely people who I have worked with on my cakey quest that have been brilliant; Katie Masters, Leynah Bruce and their crew, to Bob Harrison, Clare Holland, Linda 'Last One' Jones and the fantatic Meyer team. And huge thanks to the tremendously talented and brilliant Buddy Valastro.

And of course tremendous gratitude to all of my customers, social media followers and readers of my books for all of your support and sharing.

Juliet Sear

ABOUT THE AUTHOR

Baking expert and food writer Juliet Sear is mum to three busy teenagers and founder of Fancy Nancy bakery in Leigh-on-Sea, Essex. She is one of the UK's leading baking specialists.

Juliet has always been incredibly passionate about food, cooking with her mum from a very young age and is a keen family cook. She began baking and cake making for her son's first birthday party and instantly caught the bug for cake decorating. Through lots of trials and practice on her own children's birthday cakes (having three children under three she had many to make!) and family members, she was soon asked by friends to make cakes for their events and set up a little home baking business where she supplied to local cafes and clients. Juliet increased her knowledge and skills by taking courses at Le Cordon Bleu and Squires International Bakery school, and gained experience from spending time at Choccywoccydoodah in Brighton. Eventually Juliet secured a job in one of London's leading cake makers for 18 months where she honed her skills, making hundreds of exciting cakes. Juliet developed her own unique style and set up Fancy Nancy in her home town from a home studio and was so busy that she moved into a shop within two years.

As well as a published author and teacher Juliet appears regularly on TV. Her cakes can be found in Harvey Nichols and Royal grocer; Fortnum & Mason. She creates recipes and cake designs for various magazines and works on corporate recipe development, online video tutorials with Bakingmad.com, Dr Oetker, Renshaw and most recently has become the UK Ambassador for Cake Boss.

Her first book, *The Cake Decorating Bible* has sold thousands of copies and is published in Russia, Italy and France.

PLEASE FEEL FREE TO GET IN TOUCH AND SHARE THE CAKEOLOGY LOVE!

› *julietsearcakeology@gmail.com*
› *@JulietSear_*
› *#cakeology*

INDEX

〜〜〜

A

acetate paper 158
Acid Brights Buttercream Cake 108–13
airbrushing 80–1
anemones 128
animal shapes 146–51
anthuriums 131

B

badgers 148, 151
baking equipment 14–16
baking parchment 158
Belgian chocolate brownie torte cake
  209
Belgian chocolate ganache
  buttercream 218
Belgian white chocolate roll-out paste
  223
birds: *Painted & Printed Birds* 84–7
biscuits *see* cookies
bleeding 158
bloom 158
brush embroidery 158, 194
bunnies 149, 151
butter 161
buttercream
  Belgian chocolate ganache
    buttercream 218
  colouring 109–10, 112–13
  filling and covering cakes with
    168–71
  fresh raspberry & strawberry
    buttercream 216
  lemon buttercream 218
  meringue buttercream 221
  orange buttercream 216
  Oreo crush buttercream 221
  ruffle buttercream 96–7
  salted caramel buttercream 218
  vanilla bean buttercream 216–18

C

cake balls 114
cake building 178–85
  icing cake drums 182–5
  stacking tiered cakes with dowels
    178–81
cake lace 158, 194
'candy stripe' piping 195
caramel
  caramel sponge 204
  caramel syrup 204
  homemade salted caramel sauce
    219
  salted caramel buttercream 218
Celebrookies 68–71
chevron template 49
chocolate *see also* Cocoform
  Belgian chocolate brownie torte
    cake 209
  Belgian chocolate ganache
    buttercream 218
  Belgian white chocolate roll-out
    paste 223
  chocolate cupcake sponge 206
  chocolate orange cake 209
  chocolate pouring ganache 222
  Club Tropicana 126–33
  cookies 214
  ganache 90–1, 159, 222
  mocha cookies 214
  Multi-Chocolate Rose Cake 152–5
  *'World's Best Dad' Chocolate Mini
    Bites* 86–91
Christmas Kitsch Cookies 122–5
Christmas Snowmen Mini Cakes 114–17
citrus cookies 214
citrus syrup sponge 204
Club Tropicana 126–33
Cocoform
  colouring 127
  fans 131
  flowers 128–31

coffee: mocha cookies 214
colouring 159
  buttercream 109–10, 112–13
  fondant icing 177
  sugarpaste 177
cookies
  Celebrookies 68–71
  chocolate cookies 214
  Christmas Kitsch Cookies 122–5
  citrus cookies 214
  Doggie Biscuits 104–7
  festive spice cookies 214
  gingerbread cookie dough 215
  Lydia's Loveheart Cookies 62–7
  mocha cookies 214
  *Tattooed Sailor Nautical Cookie
    Explosion* 36–43
  vanilla cookies 213–14
cookies and cream cake 209
cookies and cream cupcakes 206
covering
  cake drums 182–5
  cakes with buttercream 170–1
  cakes with marzipan / sugarpaste
    172–7
crumb coating 158, 168–71
crust or skin over 158
Cupcake Bouquet 32–5
cupcake stands 183
cupcakes
  chocolate cupcake sponge 206
  cookies and cream cupcakes 206
  Cupcake Bouquet 32–5
  fondant icing 150
  rocky road cupcakes 206
  *Sea Salted Caramel Seaside
    Cupcakes* 98–101
  variations 206
  *Woodland Creatures Fondant
    Cupcakes* 146–51

D

daisies 136–7
decorating equipment 18–21
dirty icing 158, 168–71
document wallets 192
Doggie Biscuits 104–7
dowels 21, 145, 178–81
drums, icing 182–5
dust colours 99, 159

E

edible glitter 158
edible prints *see* edible sugar sheets
edible sugar sheets 104–7, 139, 142–3, 158
   chevron template 49
   gingham template 81
   Painted & Printed Birds 84–7
   spot template 107
edible-ink cartridges 158
edible-ink pen 158
egg white, liquid pasteurised 161
eggs 161
equipment
   baking 14–16
   cake-decorating 18–21

F

fans, Cocoform 131
festive spice cookies 214
filigree piping 194
flavourings 161
flooding effect 122–5, 158, 192
florist paste 160
flour 161
flower decorations
   chocolate 36–9, 45–6, 47
   Cocoform 128–31
   Cupcake Bouquet 32–5
   daisies 136–7

green & red anthuriums 131
leaves 35, 75, 131
Monochrome Chevron Cake 45–6, 47
Multi-Chocolate Rose Cake 152–5
Orchids 128
pink hibiscus 128
piping 33–4
push-mould roses 75
quilled panels 75
red star flowers 131
ruffle florals 75
Tattooed Sailor Nautical Cookie Explosion 36–9
Vase & Flowers 26–31
white & pink anemones 128
white frangipani 131
yellow lilies 128
flowers, natural 31
foam pads 21
fondant icing 160, 161
   colouring 177
food lacquer 158
formers 158–9
foxes 148, 151
Framed Insect Taxidermy 50–5
frangipani 131
fruit cakes
   Christmas Snowmen Mini Cakes 114–17
   preparing before covering 171
   rich fruit cake 210–11
fruit sponge 204

G

ganache 159
   pouring 90–1, 222
gel colour 159
gingerbread cookie dough 215
gingham template 81
glitterising 159

glycerine 159
gold paint, edible 31
guide sticks 159
gum arabic 159
gum tragacanth 159

H

hand-painting
   Celebrookies 69–71
   Framed Insect Taxidermy 52
   Painted & Printed Birds 84–7
   Vase & Flowers 30
hedgehogs 148, 151
hibiscus 128
horns 134

I

icing *see* buttercream; Cocoform; fondant icing; royal icing; sugarpaste
impression mats 21
impression pins 21
ingredients 161
insect models: *Framed Insect Taxidermy* 50–5

L

lace 158, 194
leaves 75, 131
   leaf nozzles 35
lemon / orange sponge 204
lemon buttercream 218
lettering 65, 193
levelling 159
lilies 128
linear piping 195
liquid glucose 159
lustre dusts 159
lustre spray 159
Lydia's Loveheart Cookies 62–7

M

marbling 159, 192
  modelling paste 54
  royal icing 122–5
marzipan
  covering 172–7
  panels 140–1
  quantities needed 172–3
  spacers 159
meringue buttercream 221
  Cupcake Bouquet 32–5
metallic paint 159
Mexican Skull 118–21
mini cakes
  Christmas Snowmen Mini Cakes
    114–17
  *'World's Best Dad' Chocolate Mini
    Bites* 86–91
mocha cookies 214
Monochrome Chevron Cake 44–9
moulds 160
Multi-Chocolate Rose Cake 152–5
mushroom models 149, 151

N

Not-so-Dirty Burger 78–83
nozzles 19, 160
  leaf 35
  petal 33–4, 35

O

Old School Trainer 56–61
oranges
  citrus syrup 204
  orange buttercream 216
  orange sponge 204
Orchids 128
Oreo crush buttercream 221
owls 149, 151

P

paint, edible
  gold 31
  metallic 159
paintbrushes 21
Painted & Printed Birds 84–7
painting *see* airbrushing; brush
  embroidery; hand-painting
palette knife 159
paper 158 *see also* edible sugar sheets
  acetate paper 158
  baking parchment 46–9, 158
parchment paper 46–9, 158
paste colouring 159
pearls 160, 193
petals
  modelling chocolate 36–9
  petal nozzles 33–4, 35
  petal paste 160
  piping 33–4
Piñata Surprise 92–7
piping 160, 193–5
  flowers 33–4
  leaves 35
  lettering 65, 193
  linear 195
  nozzles 19, 33–5, 160
  patterns 194–5
  pearls 160, 193
  pressure piping 160, 195
  ruffle buttercream 96–7
  snail trail 160, 193
piping bags 160
  making 166–7
piping gel 160
plunger cutter 160
portraits: *Celebrookies* 69–71
pressure piping 160, 195
prints *see* edible sugar sheets
  projectors 18
projects

Acid Brights Buttercream Cake
  108–13
Celebrookies 68–71
Christmas Kitsch Cookies 122–5
Christmas Snowmen Mini Cakes
  114–17
Club Tropicana 126–33
Cupcake Bouquet 32–5
Doggie Biscuits 104–7
Framed Insect Taxidermy 50–5
Lydia's Loveheart Cookies 62–7
Mexican Skull 118–21
Monochrome Chevron Cake 44–9
Multi-Chocolate Rose Cake 152–5
Not-so-Dirty Burger 78–83
Old School Trainer 56–61
Painted & Printed Birds 84–7
Piñata Surprise 92–7
  *Sea Salted Caramel Seaside
    Cupcakes* 98–101
Stencil Cowboy Cake 134–7
*Tattooed Sailor Nautical Cookie
  Explosion* 36–43
Vase & Flowers 26–31
Vintage Floral Patchwork Cake
  138–45
*Wedgwood-Inspired White-on-White
  Wedding Cake* 72–7
*Woodland Creatures Fondant
  Cupcakes* 146–51
*'World's Best Dad' Chocolate Mini
  Bites* 86–91
push-moulds 75, 99, 160

Q

quilled panels 75

R

rabbits 149, 151
racoons 148, 151

raspberries: fresh raspberry & strawberry buttercream 216–18
recipes
  Belgian chocolate brownie torte cake 209
  cupcakes 200–4
  gingerbread cookie dough 215
  rich fruit cake 210–11
  vanilla bean sponge 200–4
  vanilla cookies 213–14
red star flowers 131
regalice 161
rejuvenator spirit 160
rocky road cupcakes 206
roses
  Multi-Chocolate Rose Cake 152–5
  push-mould roses 75
  Tattooed Sailor Nautical Cookie Explosion 36–9
royal icing 160
  decorating with 188–95
  runny 190
  soft peak 160, 188, 191
  stiff peak 161, 188, 191
ruffle buttercream 96–7
  ruffle florals 75
rulers 143
run-out 160, 192

S

salted caramel
  buttercream 218
  homemade salted caramel sauce 219
sanding sugar 160
sauce: homemade salted caramel sauce 219
scoring 160
scriber needles 18
scroll decorations 41
Sea Salted Caramel Seaside Cupcakes

98–101
shellac spray 158
silicone moulds 160
smoothers 18
snagging 160
snail trail 160, 193
soft peak 160, 188, 191
splitting and filling 161, 168–71
sponge cakes
  vanilla bean sponge 200–4
  variations 204
sponge sculpting
  Not-so-Dirty Burger 79–80
  Old School Trainer 57–8
  Vase & Flowers 26–8
spot template 107
spotting 161
squirrels 149, 151
Stencil Cowboy Cake 134–7
stencils 21, 136–7
stiff peak 161, 188, 191
stockists and suppliers 224
strawberries: fresh raspberry & strawberry buttercream 216–18
stripes (icing) 41
sugar 161
sugar tiles 142–5
sugarcraft cutters 21
sugarpaste 160, 161
  Belgian white chocolate roll-out paste 223
  colouring 177
  covering cakes with 172–7
  quantities needed 172–3, 182–3
swag 161
syrup
  caramel syrup 204
  lemon syrup 204

T

tail 161
Tattooed Sailor Nautical Cookie Explosion 36–43
templates 226–8
  chevron template 49
  gingham template 81
  spot template 107
texturising 161
tiered cakes, stacking 178–81
tiles, sugar 142–5
tins 14
  preparing 164–5
  quantities (fruit cake) 210–11
  quantities (sponge cake) 162–3
trims 193
triple dots 161
turntables 18, 72

V

vanilla bean buttercream 216–18
vanilla bean sponge 200–4
vanilla cookies 213–14
Vase & Flowers 26–31
veiner 161
Vintage Floral Patchwork Cake 138–45

W

wedding cakes 72–7
Wedgwood-Inspired White-on-White Wedding Cake 72–7
Woodland Creatures Fondant Cupcakes 146–51
'World's Best Dad' Chocolate Mini Bites 86–91

Cakeology by Juliet Sear

First published in 2015 by Hardie Grant Books

Hardie Grant Books (UK)
5th & 6th Floors
52–54 Southwark Street
London SE1 1UN
www.hardiegrant.co.uk

Hardie Grant Books (Australia)
Ground Floor, Building 1
658 Church Street
Melbourne, VIC 3121
www.hardiegrant.com.au

British Library Cataloguing-in-Publication Data. A catalogue record
for this book is available from the British Library.

ISBN: 978-1-78488-006-4

Publisher: Kate Pollard
Senior Editor: Kajal Mistry
Photography © Helen Cathcart
Internal and Cover Design: Julia Murray
Props stylist and assistant: April Carter
Copy Editor: Laura Nickoll
Proofreader: Susan Pegg
Editorial Assistance: Simon Davis
Indexer: Cathy Heath
Cover retoucher: Butterfly Creatives
Colour Reproduction by p2d
Printed and bound in China by 1010

10 9 8 7 6 5 4 3 2 1